IN PRAISE OF 'A GUIDE FOR LIFE'

"*A Guide for Life* provides an important service to people who are seeking personal guidance in the bewildering world of self-help!"

~ Rob Williams
Originator of PSYCH-K®, Author

"You have put so much energy into *A Guide for Life*! I love the name and I wish I'd had a resource like this 30 years ago!!"

~ Gregg Braden
Best-selling author, Nominee 2020 Templeton Award

"Wow! What an immense amount of work and love you have put into *A Guide for Life*. You've done such a stellar job. Congratulations!! I can only begin to imagine how much effort it all has taken."

~ Denise Linn
Soul Coach, International Lecturer & Healer

"I am really impressed. You have done the work. You have been able to bring all of that into your own story. That's why it's so powerful. Because it's not just you telling your story; it's you shining the light on people who helped you get there. You've really nailed it. This (*A Guide for Life*) is going to resonate with so many people who are 'looking'. That's what people need. You have connected all the dots. You've hit the key points. You've got the right tools. You've got the leaders in the field. You are giving people not only the information (they need) but allowing them to pick and choose what they think they need. It's really tremendous."

~ Dr Jeffrey Fannin
Neuroscientist, Author, Speaker, Researcher

To the souls who feel as lost, empty and depressed as I did prior to setting out on my journey of self-discovery, and to the teachers who helped transform my life.

ABOUT KYLIE ATTWELL

Kylie Attwell is an author, content curator and facilitator for self-transformation. Her skills and services take a multi-disciplinary approach based on the latest therapeutic modalities and brain science. In her Brisbane practice, she conducts one-on-one consultations and energy assessments to ascertain where clients are on their journey, and then provides personalised guidance to help change the printout of their life. She also facilitates belief change, emotional release, and hands-on healing sessions to relieve stress and anxiety.

Despite where she is today, Kylie didn't always know herself or her purpose. While seemingly living the ideal life, she battled depression, anxiety and emptiness. After ending up almost broke (both emotionally and financially) by mistaking a passion for her purpose, she started working on herself. Thousands of hours and dollars later, Kylie discovered the key information, resources and tools to identify and live her life's calling.

Kylie's primary objective is to help others avoid the long and costly path she took. She developed the website aguideforlife.com as a free online resource for others. Gregg Braden, best-selling author and pioneer in bridging science, spirituality and human potential, has lauded this site as one of the best of its kind in the world. He professed, "I wish I'd had a resource like this 30 years ago!" It has subsequently become a hub for Kylie's work and services.

When Kylie is not helping clients, she continues to focus on completing the *Build a Life You Love Workbook Series* – seven workbooks presenting all the information, tools and techniques that gave her the freedom to express herself fully across all aspects of her life. Her first workbook, *Find Your Purpose, Change Your Life*, is a guide for uncovering your life's calling to create a joyous, fulfilling and meaningful life.

Workbook #2 shares Kylie's methodology for building and embodying a vivid, heart-centred vision for your life – the critical next step in bridging the gap between your current circumstances and the life you've always dreamed of living. Designing and test driving your desired future creates the neurological and physiological inner experience necessary to transcend your current reality. The even better news? When you biochemically become the person you aspire to be, your outer world automatically aligns to match your vision. You'll soon discover that life ultimately is an inside job!

Contact:
Kylie Attwell
+61 410 564 000
kylie@aguideforlife.com

WHY THIS WORKBOOK?

The *Build a Life You Love Workbook Series* has the potential to catapult you towards the life of your dreams, regardless of your age or circumstance. It presents the information and tools that changed my life – resources I wish I'd discovered earlier.

I felt called to share these resources with others so they could benefit from my self-discovery and personal transformation journey, and that's the moment I stepped into my life's purpose and began curating the methodologies that form this workbook series.

My intention is to take the mystery out of the *how* by mapping out a practical and clear path for you to embody the life you truly desire. In my first workbook, *Find Your Purpose, Change Your Life*, I provide insight into my struggle to find meaning and direction in life. I explain why building a life centred around my passions offered temporary satisfaction, but was not the answer to creating a joyous, fulfilling and meaningful life. I then walk readers through the five activities I used to accurately identify and embrace my life's calling.

Imagineer Your Ultimate Future focuses on the next stage of my journey, which was building a vivid and emotive vision for my life. I'll explain why this is critical in a moment and how it was a game changer. To begin, I'd like to share a little bit about the events leading up to this turning point – the mistakes I made, and lessons learned.

Be careful what you wish for

I began planning my adult life in high school. For me, that meant being independent, both financially and personally. In particular, I longed to own a home of my own. I thought it would provide the sanctuary and refuge I was seeking to finally feel safe and secure in the world.

Determined to make it happen, I began saving for a deposit the moment I landed my first casual job. At university I actively started looking at real estate, even though I hadn't amassed enough funds to secure a loan, or the income required to meet mortgage repayments. Unperturbed I kept dreaming.

A couple of years later, I attended my first financial planning seminar where I was asked to list what I wanted for my life in 1, 5, 10 years and at retirement. This was to determine how much wealth I needed to reach my goals.

To help stimulate our imagination, the seminar presenter threw some lifestyle and investment questions around the room. *How many children do you intend to have? Do you want to send them to private school? In what suburb will you live? Would you like a holiday house at the beach? What sort of car will you drive? Would you like to travel internationally? How many holidays a year will you take? Would you like to own your own business? Do you want to work past the age of 50?* I was even asked to factor in hobbies and activities such as golf, with the example of budgeting for annual green fees.

Given I was single and fresh out of university, I didn't even know where to begin when setting life goals, let alone planning my retirement. I looked at what other people in the room were madly scribbling down and attempted to put together a list of all the things I thought would make me happy.

Despite not investing in the financial plan on offer, completing this intention-setting exercise did influence my future. Approximately seven years later, I'd purchased my dream home and it was located within a 5-kilometre radius of the CBD, as specified on my list. I'd also reached the peak of my career and even built a small sideline business that I hoped to expand. I had a small portfolio of shares and was researching investment properties. I'd finally purchased my first vehicle, which fitted my 'classic car' description.

Yet, despite these perceived achievements in life, I felt hollow and deeply unhappy. I wondered if there was something fundamentally wrong with me. Being a logical person I went searching for what was 'missing'. I changed career four times. Got married, then divorced. I mistook a passion for my purpose and almost lost everything. I spent thousands on books, seminars, workshops and retreats trying to work it out. But the more I searched, the more lost, confused and unhappy I became.

With hindsight and years of personal development work, I wonder now how different my life would have been if I'd known how to delve deeper during that finance seminar. Instead of writing a material-focused checklist based largely around what I thought I 'should' have, I might have created a more heart-centred list. One that truly encompassed me.

Fortunately, I eventually learnt how to create a powerful life vision that reflects the core of who I am – my dreams, my deepest desires, my tastes, my interests, my passions and my purpose. This marked a major turning point. The process of creating this vision allowed me to sense what living this future would feel like. This helped me refine and crystallise the experiences I wanted to have and to trial them, mentally and physically. Decision making became much, much easier and I gained the confidence to restructure my life.

The biggest surprise? Opportunities and circumstances began to unfold that slowly but surely reorganised my life, making it more aligned with who I am and my dreams. This is my wish for you!

What you will gain

This workbook shows you how to build an inspiring and emotionally charged vision for your future that will feel more authentic than the life you are living now. Family, friends, former work colleagues and clients have implemented the information and activities I prescribe to take command of their destiny.

When you know the right questions to ask yourself, the task of creating a big-picture vision for your life isn't as difficult or as arduous as it might seem. As you'll discover, it quickly becomes a fun and inspiring process. By the time you've finished the prescribed activities, you will have developed a soul-stirring yet realistic, believable and achievable image of your future. So much so that you'll be eager to make the changes needed to align your life with this vision.

The processes are easy to complete and will help you to:

- determine your desired lifestyle and 'who' you aspire to be
- create a framework for your 'ideal' day
- shift self-sabotaging behaviours, improve relationships and shape your future, all by changing your life story
- gently persuade your mind to accept your vision as the truth
- activate your vision and keep it at the forefront of your mind
- change any limiting beliefs that block you from reaching your highest potential and heart's desire
- communicate your desired future directly to the subconscious mind in a language it understands
- create neurological changes that produce automated behaviours and responses to correspond with your vision
- broadcast your passion-filled intention, repeatedly and consistently
- train your mind to notice and seize life-changing opportunities.

Doing this work sets in motion a powerful creative force that will reshape your life and change the trajectory of your future.

Who is this workbook for?

Would you attempt to build a house without a detailed design? No. Yet most people never take the time to contemplate how they would really like to experience life. As a consequence, they live life by default rather than by design, and unknowingly settle for a mediocre version. This workbook will help determine what is most meaningful to you and translate that into physical reality.

Completing *Workbook #1* is not a prerequisite for using this workbook. However, if you truly wish to live a meaningful, satisfying and purpose-filled life, I highly recommend you work through the material contained in the first workbook, sooner rather than later. It may well save you a lot of time, effort, money and heartache!

The activities in this second workbook will also benefit those who wish to manifest a particular outcome, such as a smaller goal or an ambition. For example, a loving romantic relationship, financial prosperity, improved health, weight loss, dream kitchen, right school for the kids, or the ideal pet. In fact, the processes shared can be adapted for any single intention, goal, desire, dream or wish.

Additionally, this material would benefit the corporate sector*, including:

- *Financial Planners* working with clients to ascertain their deepest desires and develop a highly personalised financial strategy

- *Life Coaches* working with clients to set and achieve goals

- *Business Owners* who wish to establish not only a personalised vision, but also an organisation-wide vision for their company. Empowering staff to envision their ideal role and work environment allows for the aspirations of each individual to be known so they can be supported to realise their vision. This fosters unity and success for both the individual and the organisation.

The content of this workbook is copyright protected and no part may be reproduced or transmitted in any form or by any means without permission in writing from myself. To use this material in a corporate or other setting, please contact me to discuss how we can work together – kylie@aguideforlife.com

It's never too early or too late

People well into their sixties and those just starting to make 'adult' decisions have benefited greatly from applying these methodologies. It's never too late or too early to change your life. I've learnt first-hand that life creates friction and resistance when you don't honour who you truly are.

I was at rock bottom when, at the age of 42, I discovered the information and processes that transformed my life. That's when everything started to change dramatically and quickly. The resources I found most effective became the foundation of this workbook series.

I see my role as your guide or mentor. My intention is to point you in the direction of the information, people and tools that I believe can be truly effective in helping you manifest your desired future, just as they helped me. The more you embody your authentic self, the easier and far more colourful, rich and joyous your life becomes.

The work involved will take time and energy, but I assure you the rewards far outweigh the effort required. In my experience, designing and trying on your desired future is the most enjoyable and exciting stage. Once you've virtually experienced the life of your dreams, you will feel inspired and motivated to make it your reality. I will be walking right beside you throughout the entire process.

Are you ready? Let's get started.

CLIMBING NAKED

The story of Alex Honnold's phenomenal free solo climb up the sheer, 884-metre vertical cliff face of El Capitan in Yosemite National Park epitomises the methodologies I describe in this workbook. To achieve this incredible feat, without safety ropes, Alex realised he would need to overcome his doubts, fears and negative self-talk by knowing exactly what he was facing for each and every vertical manoeuvre.

He prepared by first making the ascent with ropes. In the sections he found challenging, he spent hours mapping every millimetre, finding the most suitable route and practising it 40 or 50 times until each step was flawless. In addition to the physical practice, he spent countless hours rehearsing the entire climb in his mind, move by move, until his body remembered every crevice.

The New York Times reported Alex's climb as one of the greatest athletic achievements ever, yet he made it look effortless. It demonstrates that the seemingly impossible is attainable if you can first imagine it, and then learn the right steps to bridge the gap between where you currently are and where you desire to be. This workbook shows you how.

CONTENTS

INTRODUCTION

This workbook will bridge the gap between your current reality and the life of your dreams. Think of it as a form of 'curriculum' or 'syllabus' that summarises why creating a life vision is critical and provides the instructions for manifesting your desired future.

Through nine carefully curated activities, you will develop an emotive yet realistic and achievable image of your dream life. Then you will be guided through a number of processes specifically designed to 'try on' your vision.

Rehearsing your imagined future gives your brain and body a sense of your new life, and ongoing repetition produces the neurology needed to accept it as truth. Doing so helps to overcome any anxieties, fears, doubts, negative self-talk, self-limiting beliefs and dysfunctional behaviours holding you back in life.

Where appropriate you'll be guided to additional resources that make completing the processes easier and more effective. There is also space to record your answers, reflections and feelings as you work your way through the material.

Don't worry, this workbook isn't a theoretical text on neuroscience, physiology or psychology. There are numerous resources that cover the hard science angles pertaining to the workbook content, and I reference several in *Inspirational Resources*. My aim is to provide just enough theory for you to appreciate why the processes work and to take action while you still feel inspired.

NINE ACTIVITIES TO
IMAGINEER YOUR ULTIMATE FUTURE

Activity 1 requires you to consider and then describe your preferred way of experiencing the fundamental moments of daily life, from the moment you wake up until you go to sleep at night. For example: *Where would you choose to wake up and with whom? What work attire would you prefer to wear? What would be your desired mode of transport?* Basically, this activity aims to encapsulate all the peak experiences you have ever had, along with your deepest desires, to create a real and tangible framework representing your 'ideal day'.

Activity 2 involves writing a detailed narrative about your ideal day based on the information gleaned from *Activity 1*. This introduces colour and depth to your creation.

Activity 3 consists of selecting and listening to a soundtrack that captures the feeling of you having fulfilled your vision. Music is a powerful stimulator of memory and emotion, and the right track will help draw your desired future into the present.

Activity 4 requires you to create a short, emotive movie capturing the essence of the narrative you wrote in *Activity 2*. Seeing your ideal day in motion picture, frame by frame, helps to animate your desired reality and form the belief that such a future is possible.

Activity 5 involves watching the movie created in *Activity 4* at specific moments of the day when your mind is most susceptible to forming new beliefs and habits. Adopting this daily practice changes your brain's neurological structure to match the reality you consciously desire. It is an effective way to prepare you psychologically, physiologically and neurologically for living your ultimate life.

Activity 6 allows you to test your desired future through play-acting the character you have built and rehearsed in your mind. 'Acting as if' takes your practice to the next level, giving you a vivid, fun and positive experience, while clearly communicating your desires to the Universe.

Activity 7 requires you to take a belief-change workshop that will provide the skills to identify and overcome any roadblocks holding you back from living the life of your dreams, such as negative self-talk, fears, doubts and self-limiting beliefs. Using this cutting-edge modality, you will quickly and easily seed new beliefs directly into the subconscious mind, embedding your desired reality at an even deeper level.

Activity 8 draws on the 'power in numbers' concept to boost and strengthen the intensity of your vision using focused group intention. You will be guided through joining or forming a group, designing personalised intention statements and conducting this practice on a regular basis.

Activity 9 consists of acquiring an intention touchstone and infusing it with your hopes, dreams and desires. Wearing or handling this powerful object acts as a prompt to consciously check and modify your behaviour. It is also a constant physical reminder that your deepest desires are in the process of becoming real.

USING THIS WORKBOOK

A word of caution! Although tempting, simply reading the activities is not the same as completing them. It is called a workbook for a reason. It's for those who are serious about creating real and lasting, positive change.

Building a vision is about designing and trying on an 'ideal' version of your life to see how it fits. It's a sacred process that is also a fun and exciting adventure to be savoured and enjoyed.

It's best to work your way sequentially through this workbook as each of the activities builds on the one before. I hope you feel inspired to complete all the material, regardless of how long it takes. Doing so guarantees your success.

At the very minimum, I suggest you work through *Activities 1–6*. These will give you a clear picture and tangible experience of your desired life, and together they are powerful enough to reshape your future. *Activities 7–9* will consolidate the work by neurologically and practically reinforcing your vision.

As mentioned earlier, completing *Workbook #1: Find Your Purpose, Change Your Life* is not a prerequisite for this workbook. However, if you truly wish to live a meaningful and fulfilling life, working through the activities contained in the first workbook will save you a lot of time, effort, money and heartache!

Create time and space for yourself

The activities in this workbook require varying degrees of time and effort. Some require daily practice while others are one-off exercises. I encourage you to review what is involved for each so that you can schedule accordingly.

Some tasks will require time without distractions. For these I suggest you turn off your mobile phone and seclude yourself in a quiet and nurturing environment where you won't be disturbed. I call this your 'envisioning place'. It's also important to do your intention setting and envisioning work in the same location whenever possible. I discuss the reasoning behind using a dedicated space that has particular qualities in *Tools for a Bumper Crop – Environment*.

Whatever you do, carve out the time and the space to construct an inspiring mental simulation of your dream life and start enacting your new reality. Trust me, it's worth it!

Note: For those activities requiring ongoing practice, I have summarised the actions required and suggested timing in the Rehearsal Schedule.

The devil is in the distractions

Expect all kinds of distractions to arise when doing this work. The reason? Changing your life story can be threatening to your mind, which is hardwired to ensure your safety. As a result, all sorts of diversions and disturbances can occur as a way of 'protecting' you from doing self-transformational work. For example, be alert to interlopers, the tendency to procrastinate, unforeseen emergencies and the sudden onset of an illness. All of these are signs of your subconscious resistance to change.

I encourage you to persist, regardless of any obstructions or interference. If self-direction is not one of your strong points, it may be helpful to invite a friend to do the processes with you as an accountability partner. Joining forces with like-minded people can be a powerful and effective way to facilitate progress and obtain results.

Note: If you choose to work with a partner, I suggest reading the section titled Sharing Your Vision – A Word of Advice.

REQUIRED RESOURCES

Most of the activities include resources that make completing the exercises easier and the outcome more effective. They will require some level of financial investment. I suggest you peruse the entire workbook to determine the resources you will purchase. Wherever possible I provide alternatives to minimise financial outlay.

Activity 3: Mind Songs

Music is a powerful tool for manifesting your desired future, and in *Activity 3* you will select a soundtrack that matches your life vision. Your own music collection and digital music services like Spotify are good starting points. However, I encourage you to also explore *Mind Songs*, which are created with the specific intention of helping people manifest their dream future.

Activity 4: Microsoft PowerPoint, Apple Keynote or Mind Movies

Activity 4 requires software for creating a movie of your ideal day. Microsoft PowerPoint or Apple Keynote are suitable for the task, or to significantly speed up the process, you can purchase dedicated software created by *Mind Movies*.

If you have budgetary constraints or don't have access to a computer, you can always create what is known as a vision board rather than a movie. The instructions for this are included in *Appendix I*.

Activity 5: Inner Balance™ app and HRV Sensor

Achieving the physical and emotional state known as 'heart-brain coherence' is pivotal for influencing the subconscious mind. The *Inner Balance™* app and *HRV Sensor* is an optional resource that trains you to reach this state, helping you attain maximum benefit from *Activity 5*.

Activity 6: The Success Principles by Jack Canfield with Janet Switzer

The concept of 'acting as if' helps to reinforce the work you've done in *Activities 1-5* in a fun and engaging setting. In *Activity 6*, I reference a chapter from Jack Canfield's book *The Success Principles*, which provides inspiration and context for successfully completing this activity.

Activity 7: PSYCH-K® Basic Workshop

In *Activity 7*, I recommend the groundbreaking belief-change process, PSYCH-K®, to help overcome any subconscious resistance that may be holding you back from living the life of your dreams. I strongly encourage you to invest in the *PSYCH-K® Basic Workshop*. Alternatively, you can engage a PSYCH-K® Facilitator or Instructor, although this option may end up costing you more than the workshop.

Activity 8: The Power of Eight by Lynne McTaggart

In *Activity 8*, I reference Lynne McTaggart's book *The Power of Eight*. It presents a comprehensive yet simple explanation of the scientific theory and evidence underlying the power of group intention and instructs you in the practice. This resource helps to strengthen your belief in intention setting, making your practice more effective.

Activity 9: The Desire Pendant by artist Dawn Wonder

For *Activity 9* you'll be working with an intention touchstone to help manifest your vision. For those who don't already have a special piece I suggest investing in *The Desire Pendant* by artist Dawn Wonder.

SOWING SEEDS FOR CHANGE

'My thoughts create my reality' was a notion I became familiar with in the early 2000s. The work of Florence Scovel Shinn and Louise Hay taught me that our spoken words and thoughts are extremely powerful. Nevertheless, I became frustrated, to say the least, when I didn't see results after spending hours silently repeating statements like *I am healthy; I am wealthy; I am loved; I am safe; All is well.* If anything, my efforts seemed to exacerbate my inner turmoil. Consequently, my 'positive thinking' phase quickly ended.

Then in 2003, I began to understand why simply reciting affirmations and thinking positively didn't work. It was spiritual teacher and author, Gregg Braden, who introduced me to the idea that 'feeling' is the activating force of a prayer, an affirmation or a conscious intention, rather than the words themselves. For example, to experience wealth or love, you need to genuinely embody the feeling of being wealthy or loved for either to become a reality.

According to Gregg, manifestation depends on your ability to imagine and feel as if the outcome has already occurred – your vision has come to life, your desires have been fulfilled, your prayers have been answered. Success is assured, he says, if you can consistently generate the quality of thoughts and emotions that produce such feelings.

Inspired, I started thinking about how I could apply this concept to my day-to-day goals, long-held dreams and deepest desires. This spark from Gregg, along with resources gathered over many years from numerous personal development luminaries, led me to create a powerful vision-building methodology for my life. This toolkit allows me to consistently generate imagery and emotions that reflect my core self and match my most heartfelt aspirations.

The activities I prescribe in this workbook will similarly guide you through the process of building an inspiring and emotionally charged life vision that feels real and tangible. My methodology is unlike other vision-building or life-planning exercises you may have undertaken in the past. Not only is it lots of fun, it's also super easy once you know what questions to ask yourself and which tools to use. The even better news? By the time you are done, your vision will feel more authentic, and achievable, than the life you are currently living, and you'll be eager to implement the daily practices required to make it physically real.

You will not be required to make 1-, 5-, or 10-year life plans or do financial projections around the money needed to live the lifestyle you desire. You won't need to develop timelines and agendas. Instead, it's all about dreaming, and dreaming big! Doing so ignites the feelings that activate a powerful creative force, which draws in the events, people and circumstances that reshape your life and realise your vision.

Before I show you *how* to create your life vision, it is important to know more about the *why*. Learning the theory underpinning my methodology will motivate you to do the necessary work. Your success creates proof, which boosts faith and belief in the process and ultimately, inspires you to continue the ongoing practices required.

Design versus default mode

Most people live their life by default not by design. The reason? From the time we are conceived we begin to create a story about life, based on our personal experiences and the learned behaviours passed down from our forebears and caregivers.

The perception we develop, particularly in our formative years, influences what we believe to be true – about ourselves and what's possible. These beliefs shape the decisions and choices we make, and our day-to-day experiences become a by-product of how we have learnt to think, feel and behave.

To an infant, life operates as a feedback system. Children observe and learn from their environment and quickly adapt their behaviour to get attention and praise. They also modify or hide behaviours associated with painful experiences. Basically, they learn to behave in a way that ensures their survival.

Regardless of our upbringing and the best intentions from our caregivers, we all receive functional and dysfunctional 'programming'. Consequently, we thrive in certain areas of life while other aspects are a constant struggle. Emotionally and physically traumatic events that are far too painful for a developing brain to process cause a child to become developmentally stunted at the age the incident occurred.

In other words, your child-self writes the narrative of your life, and unless these 'instructions' are 'rewritten' the child continues to run the show, regardless of your age. So, how do you overcome early childhood programming to build a narrative more suited to your dreams and deepest desires? It requires precise and dedicated processes, combined with intention and persistence.

In this workbook I walk you through the steps to overwrite your survival programs (your negative thoughts, fears, self-liming beliefs and so on), starting with some important background information about the human brain and mind, particularly the subconscious mind. I promise to keep it as short and simple as I can, with just enough theory to follow the reasoning behind my methodology. *Note: I will go into more detail in Workbook #5, which explores the topic of reprogramming the subconscious mind.*

Power of the subconscious mind

It is believed that the mind is comprised of two aspects: the conscious and the subconscious. Your conscious mind thinks abstractly, sets goals, judges results, and focuses on the past and future. It holds a memory for around 20 seconds and can process only a limited number of events at a time.

In comparison, your subconscious mind lives in the present. It records and stores everything that you have ever heard, said, felt and experienced. However, it does not think or reason independently, because its primary job is to respond in exactly the way you have been programmed – innate and learned, negative and positive.

The role of your subconscious is to oversee all the autonomic functions that keep you alive without you needing to think about it, including your heart beating, blood flowing, lungs breathing and bowels moving. In addition, it processes your life experiences and develops ways of behaving to ensure your survival. For this reason, the subconscious mind is not easily changed.

Have you ever felt emotionally and physically uncomfortable when faced with something new or different? Or more relevantly, when you've tried to modify a self-destructive pattern of behaviour, such as your drinking or eating habits? This is your subconscious mind doing its job. Good or bad, right or wrong, it responds precisely to how you were programmed.

Unless you consciously implement methods to reprogram your subconscious mind, it's safe to say that your childhood programming is running your life. The first step of editing unwanted or dysfunctional programs therefore involves consciously creating a new story for your life or, in the context of this workbook, an overarching vision.

Vision and design principles

A vision is a vivid mental picture of a desired outcome. It's not something vague, ambiguous, intangible, indefinable, indescribable, obscure or elusive like being rich, happy or in love. Instead, it's a mental image of something you want to accomplish that can be readily visualised. For example, you might see yourself driving a particular make and model of car or waking up in a room overlooking the ocean.

A life vision is a crystal clear, mental (and emotive) simulation of the life you dream of living. It aims to define your ideal lifestyle: the kinds of people you want around you; the activities you enjoy; the experiences you wish to have; how you can serve others; what you desire to accomplish; and the type of person you aspire to be.

Having a vision for your life is essential because it is the starting point of bringing your aspirations and dreams into physical form. You wouldn't attempt to build a house without a design, blueprint or technical drawing, would you? Nor would you attempt to cook a meal without a recipe or at least a plan for the available ingredients. Yet most people never take the time to contemplate how they would really like to experience life. I realise now how essential this type of step-by-step consideration is for achieving your desired reality, and it should be part of our educational upbringing.

Creating a vision for your life works on multiple levels:

- *Practical* – It clearly defines your life design, providing direction and simplifying decision making.

- *Psychological* – Creating a new story for your life assists you to overcome automated, self-limiting thought patterns that determine the way you predominately feel and behave. Having an inspiring vision to focus on (rather than getting caught up in the drama of the moment) helps to interrupt the habit of spiralling into negativity and depression.

- *Neurological* – To positively change your habitual responses to triggering events and scenarios, you must change your neurological wiring. The process of constructing your vision creates new neural pathways that match your design. Every time you revisit this vision, you reinforce the neural connections and prune away the old pathways that control unwanted thoughts, feelings and actions.

- *Motivational* – Having a vision that excites and inspires you provides the impetus to overcome any fears, doubts, self-limiting beliefs and challenges as you make the necessary changes to align your life with your vision.

- *Quantum* – This might be a little bit 'out there' for some, but quantum theory suggests that if you can conceive what you desire, it already exists in the quantum field. In other words, by formulating a vision for your life, you zero in and lock onto that potential reality, favouring your vision over all other possibilities.

PLANTING THE RIGHT SEEDS

Twenty years of self-reflection, research and experience has led me to understand that who we are on the inside – our repetitive thought patterns, how we consistently feel, what we believe to be true about life and our behaviour choices – is a direct reflection of what shows up in our outer world. In other words, life is an inside job! By that I mean, changing your experience of life needs to come from within.

Most people attempt to implement change by modifying their external circumstances. A new job, relationship, environment or diet may provide temporary relief, but eventually the unwanted scenarios and situations reappear. Lasting positive change will only occur by doing what I call 'inner work'.

This work centres around:

- choosing appropriate thoughts, consciously and repeatedly
- managing your emotions
- reprogramming your subconscious beliefs to match your conscious intentions
- consistently aligning your actions with your desired outcome.

The activities I prescribe incorporate all these factors and will set change in motion. The following text describes the theory behind each factor, and I can't overstate the importance of understanding these principles for enhancing your confidence in the methodology underpinning the activities. It's your belief in the process, and dedication to applying the principles, that will catapult you into your new future.

Thoughts are formative

Everything starts with intention. Every human creation or invention is preceded by an idea, a mental picture or a fully formed vision. In other words, you need a clear mental image of what you want to create for it to take form.

Elite athletes, high achievers, visionary leaders, entrepreneurs and even celebrities have been consciously creating their future for decades. Olympic and professional athletes meticulously and repeatedly rehearse the actions and emotions of making the perfect shot or winning the race in their mind. In other words, they mentally celebrate their moment of victory as if it were real.

Science has only recently demonstrated the effectiveness of this practice, with the development of sophisticated brain imaging technology. Studies reveal that identical parts of the brain 'light up' regardless of whether an action is practised mentally or physically. This suggests that the brain doesn't know the difference between a real and an imagined event.

In fact, research also shows that 'thought' alone can create new neural pathways and actual physical changes in the body. As impossible as this sounds, subjects who simply imagined themselves flexing muscles and lifting weights showed comparable increases in muscle mass and physical strength to those who performed the action. (To read more on the studies, refer to *Evolve Your Brain: The Science of Changing Your Mind* by Dr Joe Dispenza.)

If we can change our bodies without moving a muscle, what else are we capable of manifesting simply by using our mind and imagination?

Taming your thoughts

It is believed that the average human has thousands of thoughts every day. Even more significantly, the majority are negative and exactly the same as the day before. It's no wonder then that we find change so difficult without the right tools.

After discovering the power of the human mind and learning that the brain can be harnessed to attain desired outcomes, I realised that personal transformation lies in overcoming habitual, negative thinking patterns. One method for achieving this is through consciously recognising negative or limiting thoughts and trying to change them. Although this method is still valid (and discussed further in *Workbook #5*), I came across a much simpler and even more effective way to positively influence thoughts.

By holding my focus on what I wished to manifest, create, experience, develop or produce, I learnt to interrupt my automated ways of thinking and habit of spiralling into negative patterns. Similarly, this workbook teaches you how to easily take command of your thoughts (and your future) in a fun, positive and transformative way.

Emotional self-management

We constantly live in a state of emotional flux because every thought and experience, whether negative or positive, produces a corresponding emotion. Therefore, if we are weighed down by emotional baggage from past traumas it's no wonder we recycle situations that reinforce our fears, shame, anger, worry, concern, hatred, guilt, despair and depression. On the other hand, we've all experienced days when we wake up in a fantastic mood and everything just falls into place. In essence, your day-to-day emotional state of being (and those around you) influences your experience of life.

So, how do you elevate your emotional baseline – the quality and intensity of feelings – to create an inner state that matches what you truly desire? I recommend four ways of practising emotional self-management.

Two of these methods are covered in future workbooks. Processing and releasing emotional trauma is needed to permanently raise your baseline (Workbook #3). Making physical changes to your life that match your vision creates an ongoing, elevated state of being (Workbook #4).

In Activity 5, I provide instructions for creating and sustaining heart-brain coherence, which instantly quietens the mind, calms the nervous system, facilitates a sense of well-being and elevates your mood. (Refer to Tools for a Bumper Crop - Heart-brain coherence.)

Finally, developing an inspiring and emotionally charged vision for your future, the focus of this workbook, instantly elevates your mood by giving you something positive, yet tangible, to focus on. It instils hope.

Every time you shift your awareness away from your external environment and enter the world of your vision, you activate the emotions that match your desired future. The greater the intensity of the emotion experienced, and the longer and more frequently it is sustained, the more it builds familiarity and belief.

It's the emotional acceptance of your vision on an inner level that creates it in the outer world. This occurs because your subconscious mind automatically attracts the necessary circumstances, conditions and people to manifest the end result based on what it believes to be true.

Changing subconscious beliefs

Creating a new narrative that you mentally and physically rehearse is effective for changing the printout of your life. However, there are now processes available that facilitate communication with the subconscious mind to fast-forward the reprogramming process. Well-known examples include Neuro-linguistic Programming (NLP), Kinesiology, Theta Healing and Emotional Freedom Technique (EFT).

In *Activity 7,* you will be introduced to PSYCH-K®, a cutting-edge modality that allows you to quickly, easily and effectively communicate your desired future directly to the subconscious mind in a language it understands. PSYCH-K® gives you the power to override any self-limiting beliefs or roadblocks preventing you from reaching your highest potential and heart's desire.

Aligned and consistent action

Clearly, manifesting your ultimate life is not all about mental rehearsal. It is going to require action, and a specific type of action. It's about making sure your subconscious programming aligns with what you consciously wish to create, rather than forcing things to happen. As mentioned earlier, it is your subconscious mind that does your bidding.

Your job is to take the action needed to complete all the activities in this workbook and adhere to the mental rehearsal and role-play schedule I prescribe. You will also need to make physical changes to ensure that you are living in congruence with your vision and who you aspire to be. This will be covered in *Workbooks #3 and #4.*

If you follow through on my action steps, you will change the course of your destiny.

If you don't, you can expect more of the same.

It's that simple.

CULTIVATING THE RIGHT CONDITIONS

Now that I have discussed the role thoughts, feelings, beliefs and actions play in changing the printout of your life, I'd like to elaborate on the building blocks for creating an inspiring and emotive vision. When I first set out to develop a vision for my life, I didn't know where to begin, let alone how to create one that really excited and inspired me. Fortunately, the task will be smoother and quicker for you as I provide step-by-step instructions for the process I used.

Build with bite-size chunks

Instead of focusing on the 'big picture', you will find it much easier to start with what you'd like to experience in one 24-hour period – what I refer to as your 'ideal day'. By that I don't mean a one-off special occasion, such as your birthday, an anniversary or a vacation. I'm talking about an average day in your quintessential life, consisting of the following day-to-day elements:

- work
- those you interact with – partner, family, friends, work colleagues and pets
- home environment
- meals
- exercise
- social, recreational and leisure time
- creative activities

- self-nurturing and spiritual practices
- self-development
- chores and responsibilities
- clothes you wear
- health and beauty routine
- sleep and dreams.

Note: You can add in other elements and scenarios until you have developed the ultimate vision for your life. In a nutshell, your ideal day should be a microcosm of your vision.

Make it believable

Your vision will remain a fruitless intent unless it is believable. Thus, it is essential that it feels tangible and achievable. Remember, feeling also plays a key role by igniting and actualising your vision. Accordingly, I recommend incorporating personal peak experiences from the past and favourite activities, along with your hopes and dreams for the future. Engage your senses by including things that make you smile, cause you to salivate, feel warm and fuzzy inside, arouse excitement and passion, or give you a sense of inner peace, contentment and comfort.

It's the tiny, moment-to-moment details that capture who you are at your core and evoke the appropriate and necessary emotions that breathe life and belief into your vision. Far more so than simply listing what you want to have acquired and achieved in 1, 5, 10 years and at retirement.

Incorporating positive memories and self-knowledge into your vision works three-fold. Firstly, it helps you picture your future in great detail, as if you are already living it. Secondly, it acts to soothe the protective nature of your mind (which is wired to avoid change it perceives as a 'threat') by making your desired reality more familiar. Thirdly, drawing on existing and established neural connections helps to quickly strengthen and reinforce the new neural pathways and networks being created.

TOOLS FOR A BUMPER CROP

Below I summarise the precise and dedicated tools needed for designing, building, rehearsing and realising your 'new' future. Each have been selected for their capacity to reprogram the subconscious mind. They range from engaging the senses and directing your future autobiography to picking a soundtrack for your life. The order and way in which they are combined delivers a complete system for persuading your subconscious mind to accept your desired reality.

Whole-brain thinking

A highly effective tool for engaging your brain and keeping your mind on task is good old-fashioned handwriting. Putting pen or pencil to paper forces the brain to slow down, focus, explore and form ideas more thoroughly than just mulling them over in your head. It also helps to enrol both the right and left hemispheres of the brain (known as whole-brain thinking), turn down the volume of your logical mind, and open up your creativity and intuition. *Activities 1* and *2* engage your brain in this way, helping to shift your perception of reality and allowing you to think in new and more innovative ways.

Activity 7 introduces you to PSYCH-K®, a belief-change process that invokes a whole-brain state. This modality is simple and highly effective for identifying self-limiting beliefs and transforming them into those that support you. Most importantly it's fast! Using PSYCH-K®, it takes only a few minutes to seed a new self-enhancing belief directly into the subconscious mind. Belief-change facilitation helps to reduce unwanted stress and allows you to address life's challenges in a more balanced way.

Imagery

They say a picture is worth a thousand words. Imagery that symbolises and communicates your goals, aspirations, dreams and desires helps you envision and focus on the future you wish to create. Vision boards are the most common form of visual aid and can be useful. Pinterest is also an effective platform for collating ideas. Screensavers on your phone or computer act as another handy visual prompt.

The tool I've found most powerful for clearly picturing my dream life is called *Mind Movies*. It allows you to quickly and easily create a short movie that visually and emotionally captures the essence of the life you desire. I provide instructions for using this online software in *Activity 4*.

Creating a mind movie works in several ways. The act of making a movie clarifies your intentions and conveys a powerful message to the Universe of what you want to experience. Watching your movie evokes the desired thoughts and feelings that match your vision, consistently and reproducibly. When viewed daily, the associated neural connections grow and strengthen until they become 'established'.

In addition to watching your mind movie, I suggest surrounding yourself with elements that represent your vision. You could create screensavers, regularly 'pin' images and/or decorate your environment with pictures that depict your ultimate life. This type of visual subliminal messaging serves as a constant reminder to the subconscious mind.

Words

Like thoughts and imagery, words are powerful and should be used consciously. Written and spoken words can easily bypass the conscious mind and slip straight into the subconscious when the brain is occupied doing other things, such as cooking, driving and working.

It is therefore important to be selective about the content you casually absorb, particularly at times when the mind is more easily influenced (refer to *Timing*). Be mindful of the messages received subconsciously from the radio or television playing in the background, or when you flick through social media and magazines. Intentionally playing an inspirational interview or podcast with positive messages would be a better alternative.

Incorporating written affirmations into your mind movie further sharpens the focus of your intentions by using concise, positively framed statements that align with your vision. Adding these messages helps activate thoughts and feelings that match your desires, while providing the subconscious mind with clear instructions.

Music can also convey powerful messages. But be forewarned, even the catchiest tune can mask words of heartbreak and sorrow. Song lyrics that affirm you having achieved your desires, whether they be abundance, love, health or inner peace, will reinforce your envisioning work. This notion is described in more detail below.

Music

Have you ever noticed how songs evoke powerful emotions? Like stepping into a time machine, sound can transport you back to an exact moment in time, allowing you to feel and recall everything as if you were actually there. Music in particular is a powerful trigger for memory recall and a highly effective mood uplifter that can be used to focus your thoughts and emotions on your desired future.

This is what makes *Mind Movies* such a powerful envisioning tool, more so than simply assembling a collage or vision board. In addition to selecting imagery and affirmations, you will be required to incorporate a soul-stirring soundtrack that matches your vision.

Research demonstrates that music elicits widespread activity across the brain's emotional circuitry. Songs most effective for penetrating deep into the subconscious mind are those that get stuck in your head, affectionately known as 'earworms'. This phenomenon, formally referred to as Involuntary Musical Imagery (INMI), is the experience of having music spontaneously appear and play repeatedly in your mind, without your conscious control and in the absence of an external stimulus.

As you progress through this workbook, take note of music that makes you feel empowered and uplifted, and select a song that represents the 'soundtrack' of your future life. Ideally, you want to choose a catchy tune with uplifting lyrics, such as those by singer-songwriter Amorita. Her *Mind Songs*, introduced in *Activity 3*, are specifically created to help people realise their dream future.

Music will also help you focus and ground yourself when completing other activities within this workbook and you'll be provided with direction at the appropriate point.

Subliminal audio messages

A subliminal audio message is defined as an auditory signal not recognised by the conscious mind. It is another method for influencing your subconscious without creating arguments or resistance. They are created by inserting positive statements set on higher frequencies and an increased speed into audio files at a non-audible level. These signals are heard by the subconscious mind, which records everything.

Using the software recommended in *Activity 4*, you'll have the option to choose subliminal messages designed specifically to enhance your mind movie.

Scent

Smell is another potent trigger for promoting memory and emotional recall. For this reason, it is helpful to incorporate scent as an aromatic anchor whenever you are envisioning your ideal life. I call this your 'future fragrance'.

We can all link specific aromas with fond memories. Choosing a scent that has positive associations is a great starting point. However, you might prefer to experiment with different aromatic triggers to find the one that represents your new future.

Old or new, the source of your future fragrance could be perfume, cologne, essential oil, aromatherapy blend or incense. For olfactory inspiration try your local department store, a boutique perfumery, a well-being or health shop, weekend markets and/or gardens and parks. If you have the skills, create a custom concoction. Basically, follow your nose.

Wear this scent as a fragrance, use it as 'smelling salts', or add a couple of drops to your oil diffuser when doing the envisioning activities and throughout your day as needed.

Environment

The intrinsic nature of a ceremonial or ritual space is important. Sacred sites have long been revered as powerful places where prayers are answered, wishes fulfilled and intentions manifested.

'Intention investigator' Lynne McTaggart helped me understand the value of designating a specific place for intention setting and the science behind that practice. She affirms that using the same space repeatedly changes the nature of the environment itself, increasing intention power and speed of the outcome.

This concept might sound a bit woo-woo for some. It is, however, supported by scientific evidence, which you can read more about in Lynne's book *The Intention Experiment: Use Your Thoughts to Change the World* (refer to sections where Lynne references Dr William Tiller and Dr Dean Radin).

On this premise, I recommend you select a quiet and secluded place that is exclusively dedicated to intention setting and other sacred practices such as yoga and meditation. Enrich this space with personal items, scents, sounds and lighting that create an inner sense of calm, presence and focus. According to Lynne, it should ideally be free of electronic items and contain plants and running water to balance the effects of positive and negative ions.

Rehearsal

As mentioned earlier, neurological studies reveal that the brain can't distinguish between an actual and an imagined event. Your nervous system registers a vividly imagined experience as though it actually happened and creates neurological connections to match.

Every time you consciously envision your desired future in the same way, you activate and strengthen the same neural connections and physiological responses. They start to become automatic, and you become psychologically, physiologically and emotionally primed for this new reality. This is exactly what you will do in *Activity 5*.

Forming these habitual connections ultimately changes the physical structure of the brain and consequently your behaviour. You automatically think, make choices and act in alignment with your vision.

Play-acting the character that you have built and rehearsed in your mind takes your transformation to the next level. Embracing and expressing your ideal self in the outer world, through vivid and positive experiences, is a fun way to get comfortable in this role and communicate your desires to the Universe. *Activity 6* introduces several ways to dress as, and act out, your future self.

The even better news?

When you neurologically become the person that you have been mentally rehearsing, your outer world automatically aligns to match your vision. Unexpected events, opportunities and circumstances will begin to unfold in a way that even the best event or project manager would have difficulty orchestrating.

Heart-brain coherence

Achieving the physical and emotional state known as 'heart-brain coherence' is pivotal for reprogramming the subconscious mind. This state is reached by shifting your awareness from your head to your heart by taking slow and deep heart-centred breaths while consciously evoking an emotionally elevated state.

Closing your eyes and moving your awareness from your external environment to within quietens your mind, causing brain activity to slow down. In this state, your mind is less analytical and more receptive to influence. Slowing your breath will calm your nervous system, while heart-focused breathing facilitates a sense of well-being. Creating this emotional baseline makes it easier to evoke elevated feelings at will, and it's what you feel and intend in this optimal state that influences your subconscious programming.

The HeartMath Institute is a non-profit research and educational organisation that creates user-friendly, self-regulation tools for achieving heart-brain coherence. Their *Inner Balance*™ app and *HRV Sensor*, which I recommend in *Activity 5*, trains you to reach and sustain heart-brain coherence.

Timing

Another key factor is timing. A fully engaged, analytical brain is more resistant to subconscious programming, tempering your efforts. Thus, it's important to do mental rehearsal work at moments when the mind is most easily influenced. Ideal times include: upon waking and just prior to falling asleep at night; when you are in a relaxed state with your eyes closed, such as in meditation and or when practising heart-brain coherence; or immediately following an activity like yoga or tai chi.

Mood

Your mood is also important in cultivating the right conditions to create and manifest your vision. Creating heart-brain coherence, watching your mind movie or reading your creative narrative can assist to transcend stress, anxiety or a bad mood. However, if you are feeling agitated or frustrated when doing any of the activities, you are wasting your time. Stop and do something else. Preferably something fun that will elevate your mood or an activity, like exercise, that will help to release any anger or frustration you might be feeling.

Support of others

Another tool that acts as a powerful agent for manifesting your vision is group intention. This involves two or more people holding the same intent to create a particular outcome. 'Power in numbers' is not a new concept. Humans have long used this tool in various forms and modern research validates the practice.

Activities 8 and *9* involve others holding your intention to amplify its power and accelerate the realisation of your vision.

Detachment

As mentioned earlier, this work is all about dreaming, and dreaming big. Concerning yourself with 'how' your dream future will unfold invariably collapses any other possibilities available to you in the quantum field. Rather than attempting to go out and 'make it' happen, the key to manifestation success lies in doing the inner work I prescribe herein, and then letting go of the outcome. *Note: The art of letting go is the topic of* Workbook #7.

SHARING YOUR VISION – A WORD OF ADVICE

Experience has taught me that you need to be careful and judicious with who, how and when you share the details of your vision. As with any 'creation', protection during the gestation phase is vital.

When you share your dreams or vision with others, any resistance, however minor, can plant seeds of doubt in your mind, dissipating the energy of your creation and initiating a cascade of negative thoughts. It might not be what someone says. It could be their silence, a look or body language that causes self-doubt.

As you work through the activities, be very discerning when collaborating with and confiding in others. Safe options include trusted mentors and like-minded family, friends and peers who have your best interests at heart but are not emotionally attached to the outcome.

TIME TO IMAGINEER

This section of the book is about taking action, and remember, reading the activities is not the same as completing them. The prescribed processes and resources are powerful and will change the course of your life if you are willing to take the time and do the work.

The journey of self-discovery strips away who you are not, so you can finally experience inner freedom. In *Workbook #1*, I guide you to find your purpose, the first step in changing your life. Designing and rehearsing the future you wish to experience is the next stage, and the following activities walk you through this process.

As mentioned earlier, it's important to do the activities in order, and ideally, you'd complete them all regardless of how long it takes. At a *minimum*, I recommend you complete *Activities 1–6*. Doing so will change your life story and keep it front and centre of your mind on a daily basis.

You might wonder what you will gain from completing the remaining three activities. *Activities 7–9* will neurologically reinforce the vision you developed in *Activities 1–6* and fast-forward the manifestation process. *Activity 7* eliminates any subconscious obstacles preventing you from materialising the life of your dreams and communicates your vision directly to the subconscious mind in a language that it understands. *Activities 8–9* draw on the power of others to help manifest your dreams. *Activity 9* also helps you sustain focus, take aligned actions and trust that your desired future is on the way.

Don't be daunted by the amount of work involved. Completing the activities will be much easier and more enjoyable than you may think. When you have the right tools, designing and rehearsing the life of your dreams is fun and exciting. You might be pleasantly surprised by what you discover and the synchronicities that unfold.

Writing all your epiphanies, insights and answers in the space provided will help build a clear picture of your ideal future, the people you need and want around you, the activities you enjoy, the experiences you wish to have, how you serve others, what you desire to accomplish and the type of person you aspire to be.

As mentioned earlier, it's important to engage your senses when doing the envisioning work. Your mood, environment and the timing also influence the outcome. Therefore, I suggest you refer to the following guidelines when completing the activities:

- Wherever possible, do the envisioning work in a quiet and secluded place that is exclusively dedicated to intention setting and other sacred practices such as yoga and meditation. (Refer to *Tools for a Bumper Crop – Environment* for more information.)

- Turn off your mobile phone and all other electronic devices so you won't be disturbed. The exceptions to this are *Activities 3–5* where such devices are necessary.

- Choose and play music that matches the activity, as per the instructions provided.

- Wear or diffuse a scent that invokes your desired future.

- Do not undertake any of the activities if you are feeling agitated or frustrated. Only do the work when you are feeling emotionally buoyant and excited about what you will gain.

- Do the envisioning work at those moments when the mind is less analytical and most receptive to influence, such as: immediately upon waking and just before falling asleep; when you are in a relaxed state with your eyes closed such as in meditation; and immediately following an activity like yoga or tai chi.

- Aim to achieve a state of heart-brain coherence. This will help quieten the mind, calm the nervous system, facilitate a sense of well-being and elevate your mood.

Reminder: If you haven't read through the whole workbook yet, you may want to now glance over all of the activities to get a sense of the territory we will be covering and to purchase the required resources.

DOWNLOAD YOUR FREE ANSWER SHEET

If you are like me and prefer to keep your books pristine, you can download the FREE *Workbook #2 Answer Sheet.* This document has been created for recording and processing your responses and will help you gain a clear vision of the life you truly desire to live.

www.aguideforlife.com/downloads/workbook-2-answer-sheet

ACTIVITY 1:
OUTLINE YOUR NEW FUTURE

*"Your vision will become clear only when
you can look into your own heart. Who looks
outside, dreams; who looks inside, awakes."*

~ Carl G. Jung

When I was first asked to create a vision for my life that excited and inspired me, I felt overwhelmed. I really didn't know how or where to begin. You may be feeling the same way. Don't worry. The task isn't as daunting as you think when you know what questions to ask yourself.

I developed the methodology below to assist you in creating an emotive framework for your life vision. One that encapsulates who you truly are and the fundamental moments that make up your 'ideal' life, beginning with a single day. My method requires you to consider and then describe all the elements that you would wish for in a 'perfect' day. Imagine having the opportunity to create a whole new reality starting from the instant you wake up.

Those who have applied this process find it simple and effective because the questions posed are tangible and relatable. They focus on all aspects of life, from the practical to the pleasurable. What's most powerful about this activity is that it helps to identify and incorporate your unchanging preferences and tastes – the meals you crave, the landscape in which you feel revitalised, and uplifting hobbies or activities. Discovering this information personalises your vision, making it feel believable and achievable.

Constructing this outline of your life vision provides the foundations for building the future you long for. It's a fun and uplifting process. I hope you enjoy it.

ACTIVITY 1

Required items:

- Pen or pencil
- *Workbook #2 Answer Sheet*
- Background music that evokes a sense of inner peace and focus
- Future fragrance.

Before you start this exercise, retreat to your envisioning place. Set the mood with background music and your future fragrance.

Create the framework for your ideal day

Following is an extensive list of questions that cover the fundamental moments of daily life. Your task is to consider and capture the true essence of who you are and how you would prefer to feel, from the instant you wake up until you fall asleep. There are no restrictions. You are allowed to do and have whatever your heart desires. In other words, do not concern yourself with:

- how you can afford it
- if it's possible to fit that much into one day
- if you are being realistic or practical
- if you would be paid to do the type of work you opt for.

Let yourself go crazy and give voice to your wildest dreams!

Helpful hints

- You don't have to answer every question. They are merely prompts to get you thinking and feeling. Some of my 'ideal day' answers and those of others are included to trigger ideas.

- Completing this activity might prompt you to think of a number of different scenarios for the same situation. I encourage you to write down all your insights.

- There is additional space at the end of the activity to add any fundamental moments not accounted for, so feel free to add your own.

- The questions are ordered according to a 'typical' day. However, you may choose to answer them based on the structure of your ideal day. For example, you could be a night owl who prefers to work into the wee hours of the morning and eat breakfast at dinner time.

- As you work through this activity, you will notice that I load the front half of your ideal day with lots of detail. This is intentional as most people find these questions fun and easy to answer, and it quickly establishes the setting for your new paradigm. It also works to evoke soul-stirring emotions. As mentioned earlier, feeling is the activating ingredient. If you know yourself well enough, I encourage you to reproduce that level of detail for all remaining elements of your day.

Now, take your time and answer the framing questions as honestly and thoughtfully as you can. Record your answers in the space provided below. *Note: This information will be needed for completing* Activity 2.

Upon waking

Let's start with the basics. The easy bits first. If you were granted your deepest desires, where and with whom would you wish to wake up? Remember, it's your ideal day and there are no restrictions, so dream and dream big. The categories and questions below will help tease out crucial information to imagineer your ultimate future.

Landscape

In what environment do you feel uplifted, at peace and at home? Is it urban or rural? Man-made or natural? Do you feel most alive in the mountains? Or would you prefer to live in the rainforest among trees? Do you find beauty in the harshness of a desert landscape? Do you dream of living on a farm? Or is a bustling urban scene more your thing? Does a village setting call you? Do you like to be close to water? If so, is it a waterfall, ocean, lake, river, canal or creek?

- Describe your favourite landscape and the view that greets you upon waking.

EXAMPLE: For me, it is rolling green hills overlooking the ocean in the distance, and mountains to the rear.

Time of day

Are you an early bird who loves to get up at the crack of dawn? Or are you a night owl who loves to stay up late and sleep in?

- What time of day do you naturally wake up, and how would you like to feel in that moment?

_____

_____

_____

_____

_____

_____

Climate

Do you feel most alive on a cold winter's morning? Or do you prefer a temperate environment in which you can sleep without covers? Perhaps you thrive in a hot and wet tropical climate. Or are you drawn to Mediterranean regions with moderate winters and hot, dry summers? Maybe you prefer the extremes of a desert or arctic environment.

- Describe the weather you would prefer when waking.

_____

_____

_____

_____

_____

_____

Sounds

This is your ideal day, so I'm guessing you would rather not wake up to an alarm or the sound of machinery. What about the soft purr of your cat or the deep breathing of your partner? Or perhaps the sounds of the ocean, bird calls, wind rustling through the trees or rain on a tin roof? Maybe you prefer complete silence.

- What sounds soothe your soul of a morning?

_____

_____

_____

_____

_____

_____

Smells

Do you enjoy waking up to the smell of coffee, freshly baked bread and/or a cooked breakfast? Maybe you like waking up to the smell of summer or the fragrance of flowers.

- What smells do you find comforting or exhilarating of a morning?

_____

_____

_____

_____

_____

_____

_____

_____

Architecture

Are you a mid-century modernist or a minimalist? Or is contemporary more your style? How about period architecture, such as Gothic, Tudor, Victorian, Federation or Edwardian? Perhaps art deco is more your thing. What about something more rustic, like ranch style, farmhouse, beach shack or cabin in the woods? You might simply enjoy sleeping in a swag under the stars or waking up on water, in a yacht or houseboat.

- What style of architecture do you feel most at home in?

_____

_____

_____

_____

_____

Bedroom decor

Do you prefer to wake up in a room that is open, light and airy or dark and moody? Is it sparsely decorated or filled with homely reminders? Is it bright and colourful, or do you prefer a neutral palette? Is the room simple but cosily decorated? Perhaps it has a coastal, holiday feel, or it is more reminiscent of an inner-city boutique hotel. Are the textures and finishes natural, industrial or modern? Is the decor opulent and refined or relaxed and casual?

- Do you dream of waking up in a particular type of room and décor? If so, what does it look like?

_____

_____

_____

_____

_____

Do you prefer to wake up under a sheet, blanket or duvet? Is the bed soft, firm or hard? Do you have a favourite pillow?

- Describe your favourite bedroom furnishings.

Who you wake up with

Do you enjoy waking up alone or in the arms of a lover or life partner? Are you greeted by your favourite pet the moment you open your eyes? Or perhaps it's the smiling face of your child or grand baby who has climbed into bed with you.

- Who do you dream of waking up next to?

How you wake up

Are you one of those people who likes to jump out of bed and into the shower the instant you wake? Or would you prefer to stretch, yawn, roll over and go back to sleep for a few more minutes or another hour?

- How do you like to wake up?

Starting the day

What you like to do first thing

Are you the type of person who is eager to get on with their day? Or would you enjoy a cup of tea in bed with your beloved? Perhaps you slip straight into a spiritual practice like meditation or stream of consciousness journaling. Is there an activity you would thoroughly enjoy doing first thing in the morning, such as playing a round of golf, an early run, swim, cycle or horse ride? Maybe you prefer to make love the moment you start to stir. Do you peer out of the window to ponder what the day might bring? Or do you check the weather to know how to dress for the day?

- How would you like to start your day?

_____

_____

_____

_____

_____

_____

Breakfast

Are you someone who skips breakfast? Or do you believe it's the most important meal of the day and you can't function without it? Are you a juicer or shaker? Or do you enjoy a hot breakfast? Do you like to eat on the run, or love to sit and read the paper over a bowl of muesli? Do you prefer to eat breakfast on your own or in the company of others? Perhaps you like to cook your own eggs to perfection or enjoy dining out. Does your beloved whip up breakfast in bed for you? Or is it a combined effort?

- What would make up your ideal breakfast? Include adjectives to describe the taste, texture and your surroundings.

EXAMPLE: I have several favourites depending on how I'm feeling and the time of year. My go-to is Vegemite on toasted Turkish bread or Ciabatta, with lashings of butter. I also love bacon and avocado on toast with a squeeze of lime from my local cafe. If I'm really hungry, or the serve is quite small, I'll indulge in a side of grilled halloumi and sautéed mushrooms. Sometimes I make myself a bowl of fresh fruit with yoghurt. Depending on how I'm feeling, I might add this on top of Bircher muesli. In winter, I don't mind a bowl of porridge made on milk with a dash of cinnamon.

_____

_____

_____

_____

_____

_____

_____

_____

_____

_____

Preferred attire

This exercise focuses on your preferred attire for a typical workday. Do you have a favourite outfit? One that fits well, feels good on your body and skin, is extremely comfortable and makes you feel empowered when you wear it. It doesn't need to be 'what is expected'. It's all about how you feel in it. If you can rock it, you should wear it.

- Describe this outfit and how it makes you feel. What colour is it and what is it made of?

_____

_____

_____

_____

_____

_____

_____

_____

Chores

Yes, even your ideal day involves chores. Do you need to make lunches in the morning? Or start a load of washing? Do you drop the kids or pets off before work?

- Describe any chores you need to do during any given day. In doing so, imagine how they can be fun and easy to complete.

EXAMPLE: My friend Fiona likes to put on music and dance when she's doing the housework. She tells me she also loves shopping, particularly visiting a high-quality fruit store or market.

_____

_____

_____

_____

_____

_____

_____

Exercise

Exercise is both good for your physical health and important for creating and maintaining a positive mental and emotional state. It can even help those who suffer from conditions such as depression and anxiety. It also improves sleep quality and memory, relieves stress and boosts your immune system. Above all, exercise that's fun is the aim.

Do you prefer to exercise in the morning, afternoon or evening? If in the morning, do you walk your dog or go for a run to mentally prepare for the day? Or perhaps you prefer an afternoon session at the gym or an evening stroll along the river. Do you feel free and revitalised when you swim? Do you love the competition of a fast basketball game? Or the feeling of being centred following a yoga or Pilates class?

- What sort of exercise do you prefer doing and when?

EXAMPLE: *If I could horse ride every day, I'd be one very happy woman.*

- How does it make you feel and what is your main motivation?

_____

_____

_____

_____

_____

_____

Commuting

Do you prefer to drive, catch public transport, walk, ride, skate or scooter to work? Whatever your preferred mode of transport, how do you make it as pleasurable as possible? Maybe you'd opt for a personal driver. Or perhaps you are driving the car you've always dreamed of owning. Imagine there is no traffic and you've got your favourite music on, with the volume up loud if that is how you like it.

You might dream of flying to work. If so, would a helicopter, twin propeller plane or private jet be more your thing? It's not about being extravagant. It's about tapping into what you've always dreamed of.

- What would be the most fun way for you to get to work?

EXAMPLE: I currently walk everywhere. When I was a little girl, I dreamt of riding a horse to school. If I had my way, I'd horse ride to work.

_____

_____

_____

_____

_____

_____

How do you spend your time when commuting? Do you enjoy a good page-turner or journaling when on the train or ferry? Perhaps you prefer listening to an inspirational interview or watching a presentation by someone whose work you admire. Maybe you savour a leisurely stroll to work, stopping to pick up a coffee and have a chat on the way.

- What would you choose to do while commuting? If you would prefer to work from home, describe how it feels to have that extra time up your sleeve.

Work

The work you do

It is important to state here that you don't need to know, or to have clarified, your life's purpose to complete the next two questions. You can still build a clear and emotive vision without knowing the exact details of the work you will be doing. Ultimately, you want to tap into the feeling that serving others gives you. For example, do you long to feel fulfilled, inspired, exhilarated, valued, uplifted, needed, satisfied and/or energised?

Do you desire work that profoundly changes the lives of others? Or do you crave an active life outdoors that brings benefit to the environment? Are you an inventive type who would love to design and build a device that makes a difference to the health or mobility of others? Do you long to spend your days in nature surrounded by animals or tending to plants? You might find volunteering for a conservation organisation or feeding the homeless deeply satisfying. Or perhaps you aspire to create art or music that uplifts the spirits of others or conveys a powerful message. If fun, excitement and creativity are priorities of your ideal workday, how would that look?

- Describe how you want to feel when you are doing work you love. Consider the sort of meaning and fulfilment it brings to your life and the difference you make to others – the people you work with and the people you work for.

EXAMPLE: I love watching the relief my clients experience and the clarity they gain when I share my knowledge, tools and skills with them. It brings me so much joy and fulfilment when I see the positive changes they make to their lives and the confidence they gain by applying these resources.

- If you can, describe your work environment and the people you work with. How do these factors impact you?

EXAMPLE: I love collaborating with my team. They are inspirational and exceptionally gifted at what they do. As a plus, they excel at the tasks I don't enjoy doing. Having the backing of people who truly get me and support everything I do gives me confidence and allows me to perform at my best.

_____

_____

_____

_____

_____

Lunch and breaks

Do you prefer to have some time to yourself during your work breaks? Or do you enjoy the company of friends or work colleagues? What about a rendezvous with your beloved? Do you sit in the sunshine overlooking the river or take in a stroll? Do you like to exercise during your break? Remember, time isn't an issue in your ideal day.

- Do you take mid-morning and afternoon breaks? If so, describe them.

_____

_____

_____

_____

_____

_____

- How do you spend your lunch break – where are you and who is with you? Do you like something light and healthy like a salad or something heartier because lunch is your main meal of the day? Describe the taste and texture of your favourite lunch and how it makes you feel.

After work

Leisure

Now that you've finished work for the day, how do you spend your leisure time? Do you take a class, such as basket weaving, woodworking, cooking or dance? Or do you head straight home and enjoy pottering around in the garden or shed? Perhaps you enjoy working on your car or bicycle. *Note: There is a dedicated exercise section above, but feel free to add more here.*

Remember, you are designing your 'ideal day'. So why not get imaginative and consider something you've always wanted to do but have never had the time or resources.

- What's an activity that you are passionate about and love to do? Do you find it relaxing, pleasurable and/or inspiring? Does it involve learning something new, or is it an activity you've always dreamed of doing?

EXAMPLE: I love creating with my hands, which can include knitting, woodworking, pottery and renovating.

_____

_____

_____

_____

_____

_____

_____

_____

_____

_____

Dinner

What are your favourite dinner plans? Is it cooking dinner with your beloved while sharing the highlights of your day? Or do you prefer to dine out? Is it a romantic dinner for two? Or are you surrounded by family and friends? Perhaps you love to cook and entertain, with an open-door policy where everyone is welcome. Maybe your dream is to have a personal chef catering to your every desire.

- Describe your perfect dinner setting. Who are you with, where are you and who is doing the cooking?

_____

_____

_____

_____

_____

_____

_____

_____

_____

_____

_____

Do you prefer lamb roast, a spicy curry that's been in the slow cooker all day or a simple salad? Perhaps an Asian stir fry with noodles tickles your tastebuds. You might be a 'meat-and-three-veg' type or opt for a vegan feast instead. Do you get pizza delivered or pick up an antipasto platter from the deli? Or do you not care what dinner is, providing you don't have to wash up?

- What is your favourite cuisine and/or dish for dinner? Include adjectives to describe the taste, texture and any emotions your choices serve up.

_____

_____

_____

_____

Following dinner

Is there an activity you like to do before winding down for bed? I'm not talking about activities that cause you to just numb out. This is your ideal day and it's important to make every moment count. Perhaps you could describe an activity that you thoroughly engage in and enjoy. It might be restoring a car, motorcycle or bike, playing a game with your kids, doing some research on a topic that you find enthralling, or spending an hour doing creative writing or painting. It could be knitting while listening to an audio book or favourite podcast. Or spending quality time with close friends either in person or over the phone. If you are a trivia buff, you and your friends may stretch your brains at a quiz night. Maybe you are more into board games and jigsaw puzzles. Or is listening to music or dancing your thing?

- What activities do you enjoy of an evening?

EXAMPLE: _My friend Fiona enjoys playing non-competitive sport with friends well into the evening._

_____

_____

_____

_____

Bed

You have already described where you wake up. Now it's time to describe your bed-time routine. How do you like to wind down? Do you end the evening with a cleansing shower or long soak in a hot bath? Or do you enjoy pampering your face and body with luxurious lotions and potions prior to bed? Do you retire with a good book or your favourite show? Perhaps you spend a few minutes journaling about all the things in your life that you're grateful for and recap on the way your day unfolded. Maybe you snuggle up next to your beloved who's already in dreamland, or make passionate love with them. Perhaps you share your bed with a menagerie of animals. Do you put essential oils in the bedroom diffuser? Do you like to leave a night light on?

* How do you prepare for bed?

_____

_____

_____

_____

_____

_____

_____

* Describe your ideal night's sleep including the number of hours.

_____

_____

_____

_____

_____

_____

Dreams

Everyone dreams. Do you remember yours?

- What dream would round out your perfect day?

EXAMPLE: My sister regularly has flying dreams, which she loves and looks forward to experiencing.

_____

_____

_____

_____

_____

_____

_____

_____

Other

Feel free to also jot down any fundamental moments not accounted for under the headings above.

_____

_____

_____

_____

_____

_____

_____

How did you go?

Were you able to complete all the questions or at least the majority? Or do you have too many ideas and scenarios bubbling around in your mind to settle on your ideal shortlist? The more you get to know yourself, the easier it will be to refine your answers.

Don't be too concerned if you couldn't provide much detail on the meaningful work you want to do or the role you play in your work life. As long as you have described how you *want to feel* when doing work that's meaningful and fulfilling, that's enough for now. At this stage, the masterpiece that we are calling your 'ideal life' is still in the sketching phase. In the activities that follow, you will begin to add colour, depth and animation. Like any art piece, you can add to it, paint over it, or throw out the canvas and start again at a later date. After all, it's your ultimate future and you can create whatever you desire.

Now that you have completed this exercise, how do you feel? When I devised this activity for myself, I was transported to another time and place as I visualised different scenarios playing out in my mind. If you experienced a similar reverie-like state, know that you have touched on and begun to activate an inspirational and aspirational vision for your life. You are ready to move on to *Activity 2.*

If you didn't experience a dreamlike state, you may need to do some further self-exploration. If this is the case, it would be helpful to work through Julia Cameron's book, *The Artist's Way: A Spiritual Path to Higher Creativity.* It will take you on a 12-week journey of self-discovery via hundreds of extremely effective practical exercises, many of which are designed to help you explore who you really are and what inspires you. This will assist you to develop an intimate relationship with yourself.

Once you have done this self-exploratory work, repeat *Activity 1.*

ACTIVITY 2:
COLOUR YOUR DAY

"Many have forged a path to greatness lit only by a vision in their minds."

~ Chris Gardner

Now that you have created the broad brushstrokes of your vision, it's time to add some colour by embarking on a creative writing foray. Doing so involves constructing a detailed narrative of your ideal day. This activity will breathe life into your vision, activating it and helping it to manifest in your outer world.

Converting the list that you created in *Activity I* into a believable story, containing as much detail as possible, is a powerful exercise on multiple levels. It allows you to gain clarity about what you truly desire while providing a tangible glimpse of how that might look and feel. Consolidating your past peak experiences, favourite activities and dreams for the future into a 24-hour period helps to emotionally intensify and personalise your vision.

The act of descriptive writing also enhances your envisioning experience by immersing you more fully in the subject matter. Handwriting your narrative versus just thinking about, dictating or typing it forces your brain to slow down, stay on task and explore your ideas more thoroughly. Capturing your ideal day by hand engages both hemispheres of the brain (known as whole-brain thinking), helps to turn down the volume of the logical mind and frees up your creativity and intuition. When you activate the brain in this manner, your perception of reality shifts and you begin to think in new and imaginative ways.

When writing my ideal-day narrative, I was transported to another time and place. I became so engrossed in the new story I was creating for my life, it felt like I had experienced an alternative paradigm, another dimension. The best part? The vision I created felt more inspiring and real than my current reality, and thus attainable. I hope you have a similar experience!

Note: As you work on your narrative, feel free to rearrange the order of your answers from Activity I *to suit your needs. For example, you might prefer to work deep into the night. If so, your leisure time might be before going to work.*

ACTIVITY 2

Required items:

- Pen or pencil
- Your notations from *Activity I*
- *Workbook #2 Answer Sheet*
- Background music that evokes a sense of inner peace and focus
- Future fragrance.

Before you start this exercise, retreat to your envisioning place. Set the mood with background music and your future fragrance.

Step 1: Create a narrative of your ideal day

Take your time and handwrite a detailed narrative of your ideal day using the notes compiled in *Activity I*. Write in first person and present tense, and describe each moment as you see it unfolding in your mind.

If you listed multiple preferences for any of the questions, such as your leisure activities, simply pick the one that calls to you in the moment and write about it. You can always change this detail later. Your ideal day is not static and will evolve as you learn more about yourself.

What you write is not meant to sound literary. In fact, nobody is meant to read what you have written. If you're concerned someone will, you can destroy the evidence – burn it, put it through a shredding device, or tear it up and throw it in water. Whatever feels right. Of course, before you do, make a digital record and keep it in a safe place.

The point of this exercise is to capture your thoughts, feelings and ideas about how you would like your life to look. Take the time to describe your ideal day with such detail and clarity that you can see it, smell it, hear it and taste it when you read it back.

To get you started, here are a couple of narratives written by real people. These examples cover the first few minutes upon waking.

EXAMPLE 1: Before opening my eyes, the tapping of our hound's claws as she wanders up the hallway seeps into my ears and makes me smile. It's the gentle signal from her that we should be awake too. I tune into the song of the birds as I deeply inhale the earthy, moist fragrance of the forest near our house, and the breeze tickles my skin as I exhale. This is the most magical time of the day.

Opening my eyes, my smile widens exposing my teeth. I see the cluster of trees outside the big wide window. As I think about the day ahead, my view dances around the room, briefly resting on the brick, timber and plant features that make up our cottage bedroom. I could stay here all day, but I don't want to miss anything that awaits me.

I indulge in a big stretch and a yawn. Pushing back the lightweight, navy linen duvet, I turn to my right side to look at my love. As our eyes meet, my smile gets even bigger; it shouldn't be physically possible. Like a well-worn pair of Ugg boots, we slip into a hug with ease and gently kiss before saying, 'Good morning'.

EXAMPLE 2: I wake up in my gel-topped, king-sized bed feeling rejuvenated and youthful. All is quiet. I lay and relish the silence within my brain, my tinnitus now resolved. I soak in with delight the view through the bedroom windows of the rolling green hills of the Sunshine Coast hinterland. I feel a sense of freedom, peace and rejuvenation. My mornings of untangling my CPAP hose and mask are long gone. As I walk to the bathroom, my body feels light and nimble. There is a spring in my step as I look forward to the day and feel revitalised from a deep sleep. As I splash water on my face and look in the bathroom mirror, I feel a sense of confidence in seeing my skin shining, as are my eyes. No more red rashes. I am healthy and assured that I can walk and work towards my goals unhindered.

But before getting on with the day, I jump back into bed and on cue my dear husband walks in with my morning cup of tea. He kisses me gently on my forehead and says, "Good morning, darling." He then leaves me for my morning prayer, devotional reading and journaling.

It is time for me. My brain no longer has fibro fog and I enjoy writing my thoughts and memories peacefully. I'm excited as I form some thoughts already to include in my memoir writing later in the day.

When I have finished, I walk to the kitchen where my beloved has made me banana and egg pancakes, with a dob of coconut yoghurt and a splash of maple syrup ... along with another cup of tea. I feel loved. We enjoy a warm hug and then breakfast together, eating outside in our courtyard, surrounded by the greenery and colours of my husband's many potted plants. I feel at peace.

Now it's your turn. In the space below, write a story about your ideal day. If you have any trouble getting started, try drawing spirals with your non-dominant hand. This is an art therapy technique used to unlock creativity, shared with me by my friend Debroha.

Note: You may not require all the lines listed below. Use as many as you need and add more if necessary.

_____

_____

_____

_____

_____

_____

_____

_____

_____

_____

_____

_____

Step 2: **Create an intention summary**

Now that you have finished your creative narrative, write a few paragraphs that summarise the essence of your ideal day. You will use this intention summary in *Activity 9* and the *Rehearsal Schedule*.

The following intention summary example pertains to *Example I* in *Step I*.

I wake up, rested and excited for the day ahead. I don't want to miss out on any of it. My husband and I walk in the forest and by the lake with our hound, and we laugh at her princess-like antics. On our return we enjoy a fresh fruit breakfast, toast and coffee together. Reflecting on how we start our day, I smile.

I work from home, and my work allows me to express my creativity and contribute to the world. This makes my heart feel big in my chest. I smile down at my hound, who sleeps in unusual positions while I work.

For lunch, I'll jump in my beloved mini and head to my local café, where I know all the staff, to meet a dear friend. We laugh, chat and I enjoy my favourite meal on the menu.

Later, I enjoy working on my current project before an afternoon walk with our hound. I meet my husband after he finishes work for a dance class. We're working through the beginner classes to see which one we want to master, since I finally transformed my two left feet into compatible partners.

When we arrive home, we prepare and sit down for a hearty meal. After dinner we tidy and then retire to our lounge room to continue working away on a puzzle. Talking, laughing and listening to chill-out tunes.

Satisfied with the day, I shower and prepare for bed. I read another chapter of the novel I'm engrossed in before wishing my husband sweet dreams and falling into a restful slumber.

Now it's your turn, craft your intention summary.

How did you go?

Completing this activity left me in a daydream or reverie-like state. The life I had described on paper felt more like me than the life I was living at the time. It felt so real and so right that it helped me believe it was possible to live the lifestyle I had just portrayed. It lifted my spirits and inspired me to make the necessary changes. Is this how you feel?

If you were bored, nonchalant or frustrated during the process, you have not achieved the desired outcome. I recommend you stop and come back to it later. If you are not uplifted on your second attempt, I highly recommend you repeat *Activity 1* and reconsider your answers. Once you have, repeat *Activity 2.*

Journal your feelings

Take a moment to notice how you feel having completed this activity and use the space below to describe the emotions you are experiencing. Are there any immediate changes you would like to make to your daily routine? If so, write them down. This will be useful to refer to or reflect on later.

_____

_____

_____

_____

_____

_____

_____

_____

ACTIVITY 3:
COMPOSE YOUR NEW LIFE

"Music touches us emotionally,
where words alone can't."

~ *Johnny Depp*

REQUIRED RESOURCE:
Mind Songs by Amorita – www.makingsoundmatter.com/store

If your life vision were made into a musical or movie, what would it sound like? Music is a powerful trigger for memory recall and a highly effective mood enhancer. In this activity you will use melody and lyrics to stimulate the thoughts and emotions of your desired future.

Have you been taking notice of songs that touch you emotionally while progressing through this workbook? Did you identify any that make you feel empowered and uplifted? If not, then now is your chance to get serious about selecting a song that represents the 'soundtrack' of your future life.

Choosing a favourite song that invokes fond memories from the past is a great starting point. However, you might consider selecting a fresh song that is dedicated to manifesting your life vision. Listening to familiar songs can be like stepping into a time machine that transports you back to an exact moment, allowing you to feel and recall everything as if you were actually there – and this is not always positive. The aim is to catapult you into a *new* future, the one of your dreams.

Singer-songwriter Amorita created *Mind Songs* with the specific intention of helping people materialise their dream future. Her lyrics describe desires having already been made manifest. Set to catchy tunes, these songs tend to 'stick' even from the first listen. Amorita has mastered making songs that carry a specific frequency and intention, positively influencing the way people feel. *Mind Songs* act like an audio vision board, helping to connect your vision of the future with the now.

If you have already settled on your vision soundtrack, you can skip the instructions below and move on to *Activity 4*. If you are still searching for the perfect composition or are curious about *Mind Songs*, then keep reading.

ACTIVITY 3

Required items:

- Pen or pencil
- *Workbook #2 Answer Sheet*
- Computer or smart device
- Creative narrative from *Activity 2*
- Future fragrance.

Before you start this exercise, retreat to your envisioning place and set the mood with your future fragrance.

Step 1: Load the website

Load Amorita's website using the following URL:

www.makingsoundmatter.com/store

Step 2: Listen to a demo

Amorita's lyrics focus on wholeness, abundance, love, health, purpose, freedom and so on. Scroll down the page to the *Play Demos* section, select a theme that matches your life vision and listen to the demo track. Of course, my favourite is the one titled *Purpose*.

Write the titles of those that uplift you emotionally and match the feelings invoked when thinking about your ideal day. You may have chosen other soundtracks for your vision, feel free to write those titles here instead.

_____

_____

_____

_____

_____

Step 3: **Complete your purchase**

If one of Amorita's compositions resonates, select the *Mind Songs INMI Kit* that includes your chosen track. Add it to the shopping cart and complete the purchase.

Each *Mind Songs INMI Kit* includes the following:

- Songs/s
- 5-minute guided meditation to engage and boost the effectiveness of your *Mind Songs INMI*
- Instructions
- Lyrics.

If you need technical support or would like to commission Amorita to create a personalised track, send an email to: support@makingsoundmatter.com

Step 4: **Play your soundtrack**

Read the instructions included in the *Mind Songs INMI Kit*. Then, listen to your mind song one or more times per day, preferably when your mind is most susceptible to influence (refer to *Tools for a Bumper Crop – Timing*). Play it again when you need a quick pick-me-up during your day. I also recommend incorporating it into your mind movie, which you will build in *Activity 4*.

ACTIVITY 4:
ANIMATE YOUR VISION

"You can write a thousand lists and make a million vision boards, but if you don't clearly feel what you want to experience, it will never truly manifest into form."

~ Gabrielle Bernstein

REQUIRED RESOURCE:
Microsoft PowerPoint, Apple Keynote or Mind Movies 4.0 Creation Kit*:
www.mindmovies.com/ultimatefuture

Now that you have created an emotive narrative of your ideal future, it's time to add depth and shade to your creation. You can do this in one of two ways: create a vision board or make a short movie.

A vision board is a collage of images and positive statements that serve to communicate your dreams and desires visually. The act of creating one helps clarify your intentions, and the end result serves as a source of inspiration and motivation. If you want to animate your vision, you can take the process a step further by making a short movie.

Movies are generally more effective at visually and emotionally communicating a message, or in this context, the life you want to live. They engage a wider range of senses by incorporating sound and movement, and making one is not as difficult as you might think.

Your movie doesn't need to capture every nuance of your ideal day and should be only 2 to 3 minutes long. What's important is that it captures the essence of the life you desire and evokes the emotion of living it when viewed. You can even create multiple movies, each portraying a different theme from your vision, for example, your ideal home, intimate relationship, career or health.

The quickest way to create your movie is via the *Mind Movies 4.0 Creation Kit**. This online software is fun, easy to use and affordable. You simply drag and drop images, videos, affirmations and music into the software timeline, in the order you would like them to appear on the screen.

Alternatively, you could build your movie using software such as *Microsoft PowerPoint* or *Apple Keynote*. This option will take much longer because it involves writing your own affirmations and finding the appropriate imagery and music, although this in itself is a creative process and well worth doing.

Are you ready to start making your mind movie? If so, follow the instructions below. If you would prefer to get creative with your hands, instructions for creating a vision board are found in *Appendix I*. If you are super keen, you can do both.

*I am a proud affiliate of Mind Movies products and services, and I do receive a small commission from each sale.

ACTIVITY 4

Required items:

- Pen or pencil
- *Workbook #2 Answer Sheet*
- Highlighter for making notes
- Creative narrative from *Activity 2*
- Soundtrack from *Activity 3*
- Background music that evokes a sense of inner peace and focus (optional)
- Future fragrance.

Before you start this exercise, retreat to your envisioning place. Set the mood with background music and your future fragrance.

Step 1: Plan your movie scenes

Go back and read through the creative narrative describing your ideal day, then highlight the key scenes for inclusion in your mind movie. Using the space below, jot down notes on how you might depict these scenes with an image, symbol or affirmation.

_____

_____

_____

_____

_____

_____

_____

_____

_____

_____

Step 2: **Choose the software**

Decide on the software or program you will use to make your movie:

- *Mind Movies 4.0 Creation Kit* – Mac, PC and smart devices
- *Microsoft PowerPoint* – Mac and PC
- *Apple Keynote – Mac only.*

I have written the instructions for this activity assuming that you will be using the *Mind Movies 4.0 Creation Kit.* The same principles apply if you build your movie using *Microsoft PowerPoint or Apple Keynote.* Whichever you choose, make sure you save your work as you go.

The *Mind Movies 4.0 Creation Kit* is available for purchase online and gives you lifetime access to the software and any future updates. Your purchase also includes access to numerous personal growth bonuses, the *Mind Movies* community and their app.

To purchase the *Mind Movies 4.0 Creation Kit** and learn more about what the package includes, visit:

www.mindmovies.com/ultimatefuture

If you need technical support, *Mind Movies* has a trained Customer Coaching team to answer any questions and help you get the most out of the software. Simply send your questions to support@mindmovies.com and you will receive a response within 24 hours.

For detailed written instructions, refer to *Appendix 2.* If you prefer to learn by watching, *Mind Movies* provides video instructions via the following URL:

www.mindmovies.com/media/tutorials.php

Step 3: Open the Mind Movies software

I. Once you have purchased *Mind Movies*, follow the instructions in your order confirmation email and log in to the *Mind Movies* software.

2. Watch the introductory demo video: www.mindmovies.com/mm2I/demo_special_fb.php

3. When you are ready to begin creating your mind movie, click the 'Create a Video' tab at the top of the screen.

Note: Most online software runs more efficiently on Google Chrome or Mozilla Firefox browsers.

Step 4: Save your project

To ensure you don't lose any of your work, name and save your mind movie before you do anything else. Continue to save your movie frequently throughout the creation process, so that your work is not lost should there be an interruption to your internet connection or your computer crashes.

Step 5: Choose and upload your images and videos

Mind Movies has almost 2000 stock images available and a small library of videos. You may, however, decide to personalise your movie using your own photos and videos, or a combination of both. To create a movie that is 2 to 3 minutes long, you'll need approximately 30 to 45 images, or fewer if you weave in some video footage.

Browse through your personal photo and video library to determine what imagery you have on file that depicts vignettes from your ideal day. Then browse the *Mind Movies* picture and video library to see what they have available. You may even decide to take more images or film some short clips to accurately capture your desired future. *Note: If you are using your own videos you will need to first upload them to YouTube. Refer to* Appendix 2.

Use the space below to write notes on the images and/or videos you plan to use.

_____

_____

_____

_____

_____

_____

_____

_____

_____

_____

To start adding images and video to your movie, drag and drop them from the 'Pictures' and 'Videos' tabs into the *Mind Movies* timeline in the order you prefer. You can customise the way images appear on the screen using the 'Transitions' tab.

Step 6: Add your affirmations

Affirmations are positive words and statements that reinforce the belief that something exists or is true. Adding affirmations to your movie strengthens the message you wish to convey to your subconscious mind. *Mind Movies* has hundreds to select from, or you can write your own. If you require assistance with writing affirmations, detailed instructions are provided in *Appendix 3*.

Use the space below to write down any words, phrases, ideas and affirmations that might help you formulate your final list.

_____

_____

_____

_____

_____

_____

_____

_____

_____

_____

_____

I recommend that you add affirmations to all frames of your movie based on the essence of your chosen image or video. Either drag and drop your chosen affirmation from the *Mind Movies* library onto the relevant image or add your own by inserting text directly underneath the appropriate image.

You can customise the affirmation appearance by adjusting the font format and style. You can also change the position of your affirmation, its duration and how it appears on the screen.

Step 7: **Choose the soundtrack**

As mentioned earlier, the choice of soundtrack is extremely important. The right music can amplify the emotions you feel when watching your life vision in motion picture. You can choose one from the *Mind Movies* library, or import your *Mind Songs* track or your own music.

Note: You cannot add any commercial music to your mind movie unless you have permission from the relevant copyright collecting society. Refer to Appendix 2.

Step 8: Add subliminal audio

You can also add subliminal audio to your soundtrack. The *Mind Movies* subliminal tracks consist of positive messages played at a level you can't hear consciously but that your subconscious mind can perceive, avoiding any barriers put up by your conscious mind. This form of subconscious programming is like adding an extra booster to your mind movie. Peruse the subliminal audio tracks and choose one that matches the theme of your mind movie.

Step 9: Review, save and download your movie

Before processing and downloading your movie, play it in full to ensure no further edits are required. If you haven't done so already, give your movie a title, save your project, then send it to the *Mind Movies* 'Processor'. *Note: Processing your movie can take some time and you will receive an email when it's complete.*

While you can view your masterpiece in *Mind Movies,* it is best to download the file to your computer or a smart device, so you can view it offline.

Step 10: Play your movie

Now that you have created your mind movie, it's important to watch it at least once a day, preferably as soon as you wake up or one hour before going to bed. Ideally, you would do both. Regularly watching your movie creates the physiological inner experience necessary to transcend your current reality. When you become the person you aspire to be internally, your outer world automatically aligns to match your vision. These notions are discussed further in *Activity 5.*

ACTIVITY 5:
ESCAPE TO YOUR IDEAL REALITY

"A dream is your creative vision for your life in the future. You must break out of your current comfort zone and become comfortable with the unfamiliar and the unknown."

~ Denis Waitley

OPTIONAL RESOURCES:
Inner Balance™ app and *HRV Sensor*:
www.aguideforlife.com/recommended-resource/inner-balance

Now that you have taken the time and made the effort to build your mind movie, it's important to watch it at least once a day, particularly at key moments when your mind is most susceptible to influence.

As mentioned earlier, the brain does not distinguish between an actual and an imagined event. Envisioning your desired future in the same way every time strengthens the same neural connections and physiological responses. Your new reality will become automatic, you will make choices that align with your vision and your outer world will remould itself to match.

The aim of this activity is to enter the world of your mind movie and lose awareness of what is occurring in your external environment, similar to being at the cinema. Below are a few reminders to help you become completely engrossed in your mind movie, which is essential for manifesting your ideal life:

- *Timing:* It's important to do mental rehearsal work at moments when the mind is most easily influenced. A fully engaged, analytical brain is more resistant to subconscious influence, thus hampering your reprogramming efforts. Ideal times include: upon waking and just prior to falling asleep at night; when you are in a relaxed state with your eyes closed, such as in meditation and heart-centred breathing; or immediately following an activity like yoga or tai chi.

- *Mood:* If you are feeling agitated or frustrated when doing this activity, you are wasting your time. Stop and do something else. Preferably something that will elevate your mood or an activity like exercise that will help to release any anger or frustration you might be feeling.

- *Heart-brain coherence:* Achieving the physical and emotional state of heart-brain coherence is pivotal for influencing the subconscious mind. As mentioned earlier, what you think about, feel and intend in this optimal inner state influences what occurs in your outer world. Reaching heart-brain coherence is the perfect primer for watching your mind movie.

ACTIVITY 5

Reminder: This activity is best completed the moment you wake up and/or immediately before sleep. Ensure you have downloaded your mind movie to your device, so you can view it while offline.

Required items:

- Pen or pencil
- *Workbook #2 Answer Sheet*
- Device on which your mind movie is stored
- Headphones, preferably noise cancelling
- Future fragrance
- *Inner Balance*™ app and *HRV Sensor** (optional).

Before you start this exercise, retreat to your envisioning place and set the mood with your future fragrance.

Step 1: Prepare the space

Creating the right atmosphere for this activity allows you to concentrate fully on the task at hand without disturbance. Ideally, you'd replicate that of a surround sound cinema, using dim lighting and your movie as the primary sensory stimulus. Wearing headphones will help block out other noise.

Step 2: Prime your mind movie

Turn off the internet connection to your computer and/or switch your smart device to airplane mode so you won't be disturbed. Open the application or device on which your mind movie is stored, so it's ready to be played. Put on your headphones.

Step 3: **Create the right inner state**

Now that your outer environment is ready, you need to also maximise your receptiveness before pressing play on your mind movie. Heart-brain coherence is reached through shifting your awareness from your head to your heart by taking slow and deep heart-centred breaths while consciously evoking an emotionally elevated state. The method below was developed by the HeartMath Institute and shared with me by Gregg Braden. It's a process I regularly use for emotional self-management, particularly during peak moments of stress.

Creating and sustaining heart-brain coherence

- Close your eyes and focus your attention fully on your heart area. If you have difficulty shifting your awareness from your head to your heart, gently place your fingertips or the palm of your hand over your heart.

- Slow your breathing (5 or 6 seconds on the in-breath and 5 or 6 seconds on the out- breath), and now imagine you are deeply breathing in and out through your heart.

- As you maintain heart-focused breathing, activate a positive feeling by envisaging a scene from your current life that evokes emotions of care, appreciation, gratitude and/or compassion. You might recall holding your newborn child or a baby animal.

- Once you've embodied these powerful and self-nurturing emotions, continue to radiate them out through your heart for a minimum of I to 5 minutes*. If your mind begins to wander, simply return your attention to breathing in and out through your heart.

*To ensure you have reached the state of heart-brain coherence, I recommend you download the Inner Balance™ app, developed by the HeartMath Institute, and purchase their Heart Rate Variability

(HRV) Sensor. *This technology trains you to achieve and sustain heart-brain coherence and is available for Apple and Android smart devices. To learn more and find a local distributor, visit:*

www.aguideforlife.com/recommended-resource/inner-balance.

Step 4: **Watch your mind movie**

1. Once you have reached heart-brain coherence, slowly open your eyes and press play on your mind movie.

2. Watch your movie while continuing heart-centred breathing.

3. As each scene unfolds, allow yourself to feel the emotions of living your ideal life.

Step 5: **Listen to your mind movie soundtrack**

1. When the movie finishes and while your emotions are still elevated, press play again.

2. This time slowly close your eyes and listen to just the soundtrack. Bask in the feelings activated from watching your movie and allow snippets from it to replay in your mind's eye.

3. When the soundtrack ends, continue heart-centred breathing for another 1 to 5 minutes. Then gradually bring your awareness back into your body, and then back into the room. Slowly open your eyes.

Step 6: Take a break from your current reality

Throughout the day, treat yourself to an uplifting and restorative break from your current reality by tapping back into the feelings of your new future. Doing so has a two-fold effect. Firstly, entering this alternate reality will instantly lift your spirits and help to alleviate any stress or anxiety you may be experiencing. Secondly, regularly revisiting your ideal day fast-forwards the manifestation process.

1. Simply close your eyes and envision a favourite scene from your mind movie or creative narrative, with or without your soundtrack. Embody the feeling of already living this new future and maintain this state for as long as possible.

2. Open your eyes and continue on with your day.

3. Repeat whenever the opportunity or need arises.

When I was working in the frenetic world of event management, I used to make the most of toilet stops to do this exercise. It was the only moment I was pretty much guaranteed of having a few minutes to myself, without distractions and without the chaos and pressure of my work environment. It was surprising how restored I felt after this short 'mental holiday'. It allowed me to face any drama that was unfolding in my day, knowing that there was a much better and more nurturing life just around the corner.

Step 7: Repeat

Repeat *Steps 1–6* daily.

How did you go?

Were you able to transcend your reality and immerse yourself in the life you desire? Did you reach a level of emotional intensity that made your vision feel real and achievable?

Dr Joe Dispenza, a leading authority on the brain, the mind, the body and consciousness, believes that once you can visually recall the details of your mind movie whenever you hear the soundtrack, you have formed enough neural connections for your desires to manifest. This event, he says, is a sure sign that what you want is already on its way. If you would like to learn more about Dr Joe's work, refer to *Inspirational Resources*.

If you weren't able to immerse yourself in this activity, you may need to engage in a hobby or exercise that elevates your mood prior to repeating the activity. Alternatively, revisit *Activities 1–3* and then make some edits to your mind movie.

Journal your feelings

Take a moment to notice how you feel having completed this activity and use the space below to describe your experience. This will be useful to refer to or reflect on later.

ACTIVITY 6:
ACT AS IF

"Act as though I am, and I will Be."

~ Earnest Holmes

OPTIONAL RESOURCES:
Principle 12 of *The Success Principles: How to Get from Where You Are to Where You Want to Be* by Jack Canfield with Janet Switzer. (Pub: HarperCollins Publishers; 1 ed; 2005) Available in print and audio.

The next step in building a life you love is to act it out. Rather than just mentally rehearsing your ideal life, it's now time for you to be both the playwright and lead actor. Role play is a powerful and fun tool for activating and reinforcing the neural pathways formed through completing *Activities 1–5.*

If you are serious about creating your desired future, you will need to embrace and express your ideal self. Stepping into this role, even if only for a few hours, provides the ideal setting for you to test out your new future.

This activity can be likened to the way an actor prepares for a new role. The most memorable performances result when an actor truly embodies all the nuances of their character – physicality, language and persona – particularly when these are vastly different to the actor's own traits.

Fortunately, you shouldn't have to go to the same extremes because the character you will be playing is who you are at your core. However, it's still a role that you, and those around you, need to get comfortable with. The best way to do this is by trying on the person you aspire to be and the circumstances you wish to experience in a theatrical-like setting.

Dressing up and play-acting your future self adds depth to the character you have built and rehearsed in your mind. 'Acting as if' takes it to the next level by giving you vivid and positive experiences in a fun environment, while clearly communicating your desires to the Universe.

This concept of 'acting as if' is recommended by numerous New Thought teachers. In this activity I draw specifically on the *Principle 12* chapter in Jack Canfield's book *The Success Principles*. It neatly encapsulates this methodology in a fun and practical manner, and references personal experiences from his life and that of others.

I recommend the following three stages of role play, depending on your budget and how well it works for you:

1. Dress and act the part.
2. Role-play with a counterpart.
3. Celebrate as your future self.

This activity will walk you through each stage in turn. You may choose to focus specifically on your personal, professional and/or philanthropic aspect of future self.

Note: If you are an avid reader like me, you might enjoy reading all of The Success Principles *as it outlines timeless principles used by successful people throughout history, some of which overlap with the theories I discuss in my* Build a Life Workbook Series. *In saying that, I advise you to keep it simple for now and only explore this resource when instructed to do so or when you've finished working your way through the entire workbook.*

ACTIVITY 6

Required items:

- Pen or pencil
- *Workbook #2 Answer Sheet*
- Highlighter for making notes.

Essential preliminary reading

Read the chapter titled *Principle 12 – Act As If* in *The Success Principles* by Jack Canfield with Janet Switzer. It's only around eight pages long, but the details and ideas contained within could literally change your life.

Take note of the following examples Jack Canfield references as they will provide inspiration for successfully completing this activity:

- Bank manager
- International consultant
- University mates, Fred Couples and Jim Nantz
- Millionaire cocktail party
- Come as you will be in five years from now party.

Stage 1: **Dress and act the part**

This first stage of the 'acting' exercise is derived from the 'bank manager' example. I recommend you start by play-acting someone you admire personally, professionally and/or philanthropically. The person should have some of the traits that you envisage for your ideal self.

It's important to choose someone with a similar personality. For example, if you are an introvert, you will find it difficult to emulate the qualities of an extravert. This exercise is not about being who you are *not*. It's about becoming more comfortable with who you truly are at your core.

Start by choosing someone dead or alive who you wish to emulate. What is it about them that you admire? It could be one trait or several, such as the following:

- How they treat others
- Leadership qualities
- Communication skills
- Financial success
- Fulfilling career
- Family circumstances
- Diversity and quality of friendships
- Health and well-being
- Parenting skills
- Transfer of knowledge
- Mentoring abilities
- Appreciation of nature
- Connection with animals
- Devotion to philanthropy.

If one person doesn't have all the traits you wish to embody, you could base the model of your future self on multiple people.

Using the table provided, list the person/s and the qualities you have identified. Next, consider how this person thinks, dresses, communicates, behaves and/or feels as a master of the quality or qualities. How could you act out these components? Add your responses to the table.

I've provided examples of three different qualities possessed by well-known individuals to assist you in completing the table.

Person	Traits/ Qualities	Components (think, dress, communicate, behave, feel)	Your Actions
Chris Hemsworth	Health and well-being	*Dress* – fitness attire. *Behaviour* – consume healthy diet, daily exercise. *Feel* – fit, strong, trim, energised and clear minded.	• Wear fitness attire that you look good and feel comfortable in. • Eat unprocessed foods and follow an exercise routine that you enjoy. • Mentally rehearse the sensation of being fit and healthy.
Elon Musk	Financial success	*Think* – entrepreneurial and problem-solving mindset. *Communicate* – clear, direct, inquisitive. *Feel* – optimistic, prosperous, assured, generous.	• Identify opportunities and problems to solve. • Ask everyone you meet their five best ideas. • Mentally rehearse the sensation of being able to purchase whatever you like, whenever you like.
Marie Curie	Fulfilling career	*Think* – open, inquisitive and analytical mindset. *Behaviour* – driven, hardworking, focused. *Feel* – fortunate, inspired, curious, determined.	• Constantly seek understanding through questioning. • Learn something new every day. • Rehearse mentally the sensation of making a life-changing discovery.

Person	Traits/ Qualities	Components (think, dress, communicate, behave, feel)	Your Actions

Now that you have done the hard stuff, it's time for some fun. Identify where, when and how you will incorporate 'your actions' into day-to-day life. It's about trying on one facet of your future self at a time until it becomes second nature. You might even have to learn a new skill to adopt a specific trait.

Make the most of everyday moments to role-play these traits. It might be when you are driving, walking to work, catching public transport, waiting for a friend or standing in line at the grocery store. If you aspire to be fit and healthy, you could emulate the way a fitness guru moves when you are out for an afternoon stroll. Or, while doing the grocery shopping, imagine what would be in your basket if money wasn't an issue. Instead of scrolling through social media or checking emails, think of a problem you wish to solve and take the time to start researching a solution.

Stage 2: Role-play with a counterpart

This second stage of the 'acting' exercise draws on the 'university mates' example from *The Success Principles*.

Kids are excellent at imaginary role play. You might want to observe some in action to get a feel for it and help you decide the right partner or partners to join your 'play'.

Start by determining what aspect of your ideal life you would like to focus on – personal, professional or philanthropic. For example, if you are a 35-year-old single woman and long to be married with a family, you might prioritise role-playing a wife with two children. If your personal life is on track, but you have always dreamed of being a crocodile handler, you could focus on role-playing your true career aspirations.

The next step is finding the right person to play-act your counterpart. Ideally, you would pair up with a family member, friend or work colleague whose aspirations are the perfect complement to yours. If there is no one suitable in your circle, or you would prefer to keep your intentions on the quiet for now, perhaps you could rehearse with an aspiring actor.

You can role-play any aspect of your desires you care to, as often as you like. The key is to act out your ideal scenario as if you were already 'living the dream'. Below are some example personal, professional and philanthropic role-play exercises to help get you started:

Personal

Children often spend hours role-paying their dream future with friends. They can go to great lengths playing house or pretending they are a superhero saving the world, a sporting legend or a racing car driver. This can continue well into adulthood, although it tends to be the exception not the rule.

Your aim here is to recapture your childhood. Let your imagination run wild and embrace the positive habit of acting out your deepest desires.

Pair up with your counterpart and describe in detail your ideal reality as if it has already happened. For example, you might recount how you 'felt':

- meeting your adorable new pet

- receiving your promotion

- choosing and wearing your new wardrobe following weight loss

- marrying the love of your life

- at the birth of your child

- moving into the beautiful home you built

- on that magical holiday to your dream destination

- achieving a life-long goal or award.

While this list is general in nature, feel free to express your inner child's wildest dreams in detail. Your perfect counterpart will easily ad lib and contribute valuable details, helping to build excitement and bring further reality to the role play.

Professional

This exercise allows you and an appropriate counterpart to play-act a pivotal moment in your respective professional lives. To get you started, I present the framework for role-playing two scenarios: coach/mentor and media interview.

Coaching or mentoring relationship

These days all sorts of people in all types of professions have coaches and mentors. Below are two examples to give you some ideas of the roles you and your counterpart can act out. The first one is centred around a sporting career, while the second models the business sector. Feel free to adapt the setting to suit your professional aspirations whether they are in the arts, sciences, finance, construction and so on.

    i.   You are a professional athlete teaming up with your coach to replay a big win over a celebratory drink. Relive how you felt during pivotal moments of your performance, while your coach reflects on what aspects of their training attributed to your win. You might also talk about the other competitors and event conditions. The key is to stay in character and make your win as real and as believable as possible.

    ii.   You meet up with your business mentor to celebrate your new executive role in the company of your dreams. Together you reflect on your career highlights and the expertise you acquired to attain this promotion.

Media interview

This scenario centres around your future self being interviewed following a major professional accomplishment. For example, you might be a renowned artist discussing your career highlights with a New York Times art critic at the opening of your retrospective exhibition. To role-play this scene, you could pair up with a budding journalist who has a passion for art.

This role-pay scenario would work for a number of career aspirations. To provide inspiration, the table below covers various professions and the potential achievement an interview could be based around. Feel free to drill down more specifically to suit your dream occupation.

Occupation	Desired Achievement
Author/Writer	Earn a place on a New York Times list
Head chef	Awarded a Michelin Star
Sustainable architect	Deliver a 'green' community project
Filmmaker	Receive an Academy award
Scientist	Significant breakthrough in your chosen field
Economist	Alleviate poverty
Peacekeeper	Work in developing countries for the UN
Humanitarian	Set up a mobile shower or laundry service for the homeless
Business leader	Recognised as a model company in terms of financial success, product quality and staff satisfaction
Medical professional	Developed lifesaving equipment, procedure or standard of care
Photographer	On the cover of prestigious magazine e.g. National Geographic
Inventor	Create a world-changing system or device
Engineer/Industrial Designer	Design a solution for building, ecological or humanitarian needs
Educator	Inspire lifelong learning
Farmer	Develop sustainable agricultural systems
Investigative journalist	Uncover systemic corruption
Law enforcement	Solve a crime ring
Politician	Legislate change that improves society

Philanthropic

If you aspire to set up a charity or foundation, consider the beneficiaries and the scenario you could role-play, for example, education for the underprivileged, supporting the arts or scientific research, improving mental health, or preserving the environment and wildlife.

Below are two possible scenarios to get you thinking:

i. As a budding philanthropist you tee up with an aspiring lawyer, accountant or business advisor who wishes to work in the not-for-profit sector. Together you discuss the intention, entity structure, financial needs, operations and services of the charity you are establishing. *Tip: Make sure your role play maintains an upbeat and inspirational feel rather than getting bogged down in complexity.*

ii. You pair with someone who already works in the not-for-profit sector. Together, play-act the interchange of you donating money to their cause and discussing the good that will ensue.

Stage 3: Celebrate as your future self

This last 'acting as if' exercise draws on the 'come as you will be in five years from now party' and 'millionaire cocktail party' examples in *The Success Principle*. It involves throwing a party to celebrate you and your guests having 'already made it', and it can range from an intimate dinner with friends to an all-out gala event.

Being immersed in a festive atmosphere for several hours with guests role-playing their future selves stimulates and simulates an emotional experience of having achieved your deepest desires. As mentioned earlier, it is 'feeling' that ignites and actualises your vision. Therefore, the more 'real' the party, the stronger the feelings generated and the more likely it is that your outer world will shape itself to reflect your experience.

Below I list the things you will need to consider and organise when hosting your event. I have also created a detailed event-planning checklist in *Appendix 4* that outlines each party element within a timeline, commencing two months before the event. It includes space for you to jot down any notes, along with examples and practical considerations to ensure a seamless and fun event.

Consider who will you be in five years

Who would you like to be in five years? What would you like your accomplishments to be, and what would it feel like to achieve these goals?

Determine your budget and party type

Before you do anything else, consider how much money you wish to spend on your party. This will pretty much determine the type of event you can host, that is, small and intimate versus an extravaganza.

Organise a venue

Decide whether to host your party at home as opposed to a venue. Bear in mind the number of guests, the scene you want to set and how you intend to use the event space. If hiring a venue, secure your booking as soon as possible.

Plan your guest list

Consider who you know that would relish the type of event you are hosting and draw up a list.

Confirm a date and time

Give guests plenty of time to fully prepare for your party. This also increases the likelihood of securing the venue of your choice.

Invite your guests

Send out your invitations. Whatever form they take, make sure you include the *date, time, location, RSVP cut off* and, most importantly, the *intent* of your party. Leading up to the event, use online channels to build excitement and keep your guests up to date.

Book entertainment and extras

Big or small, your event will be improved by entertainment and event professionals. Consider engaging performers and a stylist to create the right atmosphere, and a photographer and/or videographer to document your event.

Organise catering

Consider the type of food and beverages that suit your event, how they will be served and any guest dietary requirements. If applicable, lock in the caterer as early as possible. If self-catering, take care of any preparation in the week leading up to the event, so there is less to do on the day. Determine final numbers one week before.

Character preparation

To help remain in character throughout the event, you might like to create an elevator pitch and rehearse it in your mind well before the day. Things to consider include:

- who you are
- what you have accomplished
- what it felt like to achieve this goal
- the major steps and milestones
- how this has improved your life and/or the world.

For example, you might aspire to help those impacted by the pandemic. Depending on your skill level and resources you may play the role of a scientist, medical or mental health professional, philanthropist, politician, advertising executive or influencer. Decide on whether you have developed/financed/promoted/ negotiated an awareness campaign, prevention, treatment or recovery support. Consider how you would describe your role in this achievement and why it is important.

Organise your costume and props

How will you communicate to yourself and others that you have achieved your goals and desires? Make sure you don't leave this decision and appropriate arrangements, such as costume and props, to the last minute. Most importantly, give yourself plenty of time to get in character.

Devise an event program and seating plan

How would you like your party to unfold? Documenting this helps inform everyone involved. If applicable, consider drawing up a seating plan to assist guests to stay in character. People who know one another may revert to their usual banter if not separated.

Venue set-up

Don't leave any prop making, venue set-up and decorating until the last minute.

Enjoy the party

Once everything is in place and guests have arrived, don't forget to enjoy every moment of your future life.

If you feel uncomfortable with the role play at first, start by asking questions of others; find out who they are and what they have achieved. This might help ease your nerves and give you hints on how to convey the accomplishments of your future self.

After the party

Keep the party going by sharing photos and footage with guests and encourage them to recap on any highlights and outcomes from the event. Be sure to thank venue staff, helpers and guests.

How did you go?

Did you enjoy role-playing your future self? Are the qualities or traits that you have observed, analysed and put into practice something you could permanently embody? Or do you need further knowledge and/or skills to feel truly comfortable in your ideal persona and dream scenarios? Where necessary, tweak accordingly and continue to 'act as if'.

It's important that you don't see this activity as just a one-off. If you are serious about becoming your ideal self, continue to play that role whenever and wherever possible.

If you struggled to complete this activity or felt like a fraud in the role, you will benefit from *Activity 7*. It is designed to remove any subconscious resistance or unease around achieving your life vision.

ACTIVITY 7:
REMOVING SUBCONSCIOUS RESISTANCE

"PSYCH-K can change long-standing, limiting beliefs in a matter of minutes."

~ Dr Bruce H. Lipton

REQUIRED RESOURCE:
PSYCH-K® Basic Workshop – ww.psych-k.com/workshop-search/

By creating an inspiring, powerful and emotive vision for your life, and then role-playing it both mentally and physically, your subconscious mind has begun to accept this new future. You will now learn to fast-track the reprogramming process using PSYCH-K®, the cutting-edge belief-change modality originated by psychotherapist Rob Williams.

As mentioned earlier, your experience of life is based on the story you have created, particularly in your formative years. To modify this narrative, your core beliefs need to change at both a conscious and subconscious level.

PSYCH-K® allows you to communicate your personal goals and seed beliefs that support your conscious desires directly into the subconscious mind in a language it understands. In addition, PSYCH-K® has protocols in place to ensure that 'changing your programming' is safe and appropriate, and that the subconscious mind has accepted the given directive.

There are two ways you can benefit from the power of PSYCH-K®. You can complete the *PSYCH-K® Basic Workshop* and learn to do the reprogramming yourself, or you can engage a PSYCH-K® Facilitator or Instructor, which can be more costly. I personally believe in self-sovereignty and therefore recommend investing in the *Basic Workshop* as it will give you skills to facilitate lasting and positive change for yourself and others. This activity is based on you undertaking the workshop.

ACTIVITY 7

Required items:

- Pen or pencil
- *Workbook #2 Answer Sheet*

Step 1: Enrol in a PSYCH-K® Basic Workshop

- To find a *PSYCH-K® Basic Workshop* in your area, type the following URL into your website browser: www.psych-k.com/workshop-search/

- Scroll down the page, past the flow chart diagram and *Notes* heading, then click on the *Search by Workshop Type* field. Select *Basic Workshop* from the dropdown menu.

- Click on the *Search by Country* field and select your country from the dropdown menu. If your country is *not* listed, select one you could visit to attend the workshop. You can also email info@psych-k.com and the PSYCH-K® team may give you some alternatives.

- You can also filter by *State* (US only), *Instructor's Name*, *Language* and *Region/Continent*.

- A list of upcoming *Basic Workshops* will appear in the results section in date order. Peruse the list and choose the one most suitable for you.

- Click on the *Registration Details* button and contact the PSYCH-K® Instructor presenting the workshop using the information provided.

- Enrol in and pay for the workshop.

Step 2: **Complete the PSYCH-K® Basic Workshop**

The *PSYCH-K® Basic Workshop* is an in-person event held over three days. Below is a brief summary of what you will learn in the workshop:

- The importance of beliefs and understanding how they create your reality
- The function of the left and right hemispheres of the brain, and how to maximise communication between them
- Differences between the conscious, subconscious and superconscious minds, and the role of each in changing limiting beliefs
- How to communicate with the subconscious mind using a unique muscle testing protocol
- Two *PSYCH-K® Balance* processes for changing subconscious beliefs
- How to create well-formed belief statements to enhance any area of your life
- A goal clarification process called *VAK to the Future*, which makes it easier for the subconscious mind to understand your goals and support you to achieve them
- How to facilitate belief change within yourself and others
- How to apply PSYCH-K® in your daily life.

By the end of the workshop, you will have the skills to quickly and easily change long-held, self-sabotaging beliefs into ones that support you at the subconscious level. You will not only be equipped to help yourself, but also to facilitate significant and lasting changes in the lives of others.

Step 3: **Apply your workshop skills**

In the context of this workbook, you can apply your *PSYCH-K®
Basic Workshop* skills as follows:

Test and balance affirmations

Prioritise muscle testing each affirmation featured in your mind
movie to ensure that you are not unintentionally activating any
subconscious resistance when you view it. If you test 'weak' for
any affirmation, perform the *PSYCH-K® Balance* process to seed
it directly into your subconscious mind to support what you are
consciously affirming.

To further support all aspects of your life, use the *PSYCH-K®
Balance* process to test and 'balance' any self-limiting subconscious
beliefs you hold. You could start with the list of goal statements
provided as part of the *PSYCH-K® Basic Workshop*. For further
inspiration, consider exploring the work of Florence Scovel Shinn
and Louise Hay, as listed in *Recommended Resources*.

In the space below, write down any affirmations, self-limiting
beliefs or known triggers you'd like to resolve.

_____

_____

_____

_____

_____

_____

_____

_____

_____

_____

Communicate your vision

Use the *VAK to the Future* process to communicate your vision directly to the subconscious mind in a language that it understands. This accelerates the outcome of manifesting your vision. Essentially, you are telling the subconscious mind what you want to achieve or experience in the future and how you will know when this has occurred.

If you would like assistance with this process, I suggest you pair up with a fellow workshop participant or engage a PSYCH-K® Facilitator or Instructor.

Step 4: Continue to rehearse

Once you've completed the PSYCH-K® processes, it doesn't mean the work is done. Continue to replay your mind movie, mentally and physically role-play your vision, and read or rewrite your creative narrative as per the *Rehearsal Schedule*.

How did you go?

Now that you've applied your PSYCH-K® workshop skills, does your life vision feel more believable and achievable? Are you starting to feel more comfortable being the new version of yourself?

If you are experiencing any resistance in the form of doubts, fears, limiting beliefs or self-sabotaging behaviour, further *PSYCH-K® Balances* will be beneficial. Identify any disempowering beliefs and recurring challenges, and then repeat the balance process as per *Step 3*. This will maximise the power of your subconscious mind to support your conscious desires.

ACTIVITY 8:
STRENGTH IN NUMBERS

"There is power in unity, and there is power in numbers."

~ Dr Martin Luther King Jr

REQUIRED RESOURCE:
The Power of Eight: Harnessing the Miraculous Energies of a Small Group to Heal Others, Your Life, and the World by Lynne McTaggart. (Pub: Atria Books; Reprint edition; 2018) Available in print and audio.

'Power in numbers' is not a new concept. The difference that communal actions and thoughts can make has underpinned rituals, ceremonies and religious practices throughout history.

Research suggests that when two or more people come together with a shared intention, mission or vision, the effect generated is exponentially amplified. This phenomenon was named the 'Maharishi Effect'. Subsequent studies suggest that focused intention on a mass scale results in predictable and measurable effects in the social and natural environment.

Investigative journalist and author, Lynne McTaggart, has spent more than 22 years studying and reporting on the phenomenon of shared intention. She has written two international bestselling books on the subject and is the architect of the *Intention Experiment*, a global scientific study involving thousands of participants testing the power of group thought.

Lynne's work reveals that focused group intention has an extraordinary effect not only on the recipients of the intention, but also on the senders. In this activity you will be drawing on the strength of combined group thought to help manifest your vision. You will work in a group of eight or so, intending for yourself and others both within and outside the group.

ACTIVITY 8

Required items:

- Pen or pencil
- *Workbook #2 Answer Sheet*
- Your intention summary, created in *Activity 2*
- *Choku Rei* track by Jonathan Goldman from his *Reiki Chants* album
- Future fragrance.

Step 1: A reading exercise

This exercise starts with reading *The Power of Eight* by Lynne McTaggart. Part I of her book explains the theory and results underlying group-focused intention, group size and the benefits experienced by senders and receivers. Part II discusses creating or joining a Power of Eight circle and the intention process itself *Note: Pay particular attention to Lynne's instructions in Part II for completing this activity.*

Step 2: Gather your group

It's not necessary to have precisely eight people in a group. However, Lynne's research suggests that there should be no fewer than six and no more than twelve participants. She also reports that it makes no difference if your group meets in person or virtually.

To assist you in connecting and forming a Power of Eight Group with like-minded people in your time zone, Lynne has created a Facebook group called 'Connecting and Healing with the Power of Eight'. Below is the URL for your convenience:

www.facebook.com/groups/1068844430161141

Once your request to join this Facebook group has been accepted, you can write a post similar to the following:

Hello, I'm located in [insert your city, country and time zone] and would like to join or form a Power of Eight Group. Thanks in advance for your assistance.

Alternatively, you may form a group with people you already know. Lynne provides instructions for doing so in Chapter 22 of *The Power of Eight*, which covers the following:

- Structuring and scheduling group intention sessions, whether in person or virtually
- Platforms to use for virtual groups
- Choosing your intention space
- Selecting an intention target
- Designing your intention statement
- The process for 'powering up' and holding the intention
- Closing an intention circle session
- Documenting progress.

In the space below, write down any names of like-minded people you intend to invite and notes on structuring and scheduling your group.

If you are invited to join an existing group, ask for information on the following:

- Meeting frequency
- Proceedings
- Group etiquette.

If you are the facilitator of a new group, you will need to establish a similar protocol to the above and lead the group. If you are not comfortable leading, one of the other members may enjoy performing this role, or you may choose to take turns.

Step 3: **Choose your personal intention focus**

Prior to meeting with your group, spend time journaling about the events that are unfolding in your life – things that are flowing with ease, along with those giving you problems. *Note: You will need this information for* Step 5.

_____

_____

_____

_____

_____

_____

_____

_____

_____

_____

_____

_____

Next, determine which aspects of your vision could benefit from group intention. While several areas may fall into this category, it's important to focus on one element at a time, in order of priority.

The nature of your focus will vary depending on the stage of your journey. To get you started, below are several intention examples ranging from general to specific:

- Being financially supported to live your life purpose
- Complete recovery from a chronic or 'terminal' illness
- Improved relationships with your partner, family members, work colleagues and so on
- Meeting the love of your life
- Falling pregnant
- Purchasing your ideal home within budget
- Amicable divorce settlement.

When crafting the wording of your Power of Eight intention, I highly recommend following Lynne's 'formula'. Below are a few of examples to get you started:

- *My intention is that [insert first and last name] be immediately, completely and permanently healed/free of all traces of [insert condition] and any possible metastases elsewhere in [his/her] body, and that [he/she] be healthy and well in every way.*

- *My intention is that [insert first and last name] be immediately, completely and permanently healed of all pain relating to [his/her] operation and for [his/her] [insert body part] to be moving/functioning normally in every way.*

- *My intention is to lower violence and restore peace during the [insert situation and location] by [insert percentage] or more, and that it may lead to [insert desired outcome].*

- *My intention is to easily and joyfully earn [insert desired amount] or more per month doing work that I love, and which feels like play to me.*

Now it's your turn, write down your Power of Eight intention.

_____

_____

_____

_____

_____

_____

_____

_____

_____

_____

_____

Step 4: Participate in an intention session

You can receive the benefits of group-focused intention on three different levels:

- Working with your Power of Eight group
- Participating in Lynne's *Intention of the Week* (find out more at www.lynnemctaggart.com/intention-experiments/intentions-of-the-week/)
- Enrolling in Lynne's foundation course, *Intention Essentials* – a live event that includes personalised interaction with Lynne and other course members (find out more at www.lynnemctaggart.com).

Note: During group intention sessions, Lynne plays the Choku Rei *track by Jonathan Goldman from his* Reiki Chants *album. I recommend using this track with your Power of Eight group. Don't forget to set the mood with your future fragrance.*

Step 5: Write down your observations

Following each intention session, make notes on how you felt during the process (regardless of whether the group is intending for you or another). For example, did you have any bodily sensations or emotional reactions? If you have a physical condition, did you experience any change in pain levels or symptoms?

_____

_____

_____

_____

_____

_____

_____

Continue to document events unfolding in your life and note any specific areas of improvement. It can also be useful to reflect on previous journal entries for comparison (as mentioned above in *Step 3*).

Take particular notice of manifestations, yours and those of others in your group, as this becomes tangible evidence that intention setting works. Such proof facilitates acceptance and belief in the process, helping to catapult you into your new future.

ACTIVITY 9:
THE POWER OF SACRED OBJECTS

"When your intentions are pure, so too will be your success."

~ Charles F. Glassman MD

REQUIRED RESOURCE:
An intention touchstone. If you don't already have a special piece, I suggest investing in *The Desire Pendant* by artist Dawn Wonder:
www.dawnwonder.com/the-pendant

A physical object that represents your personal hopes, dreams and wishes is another powerful tool for manifesting your vision. Such an item acts as a tangible reminder to be conscious of your behaviours and that your deepest desires are in the process of being realised.

As mentioned previously, there is power in having others, who are not emotionally attached to the outcome, hold the intention of your vision. Doing so sends a powerful message out to the Universe on your behalf.

In this activity you will combine these two practices by selecting a touchstone as the receptacle for your vision, and then infusing it with intention. Wearing or handling your touchstone becomes a daily prompt to align your thoughts, words, emotions and actions with your deepest desires.

You may choose to infuse a treasured object already in your possession, preferably one associated with fond memories. Alternatively, you could purchase a piece from someone such as Dawn Wonder, an artist who specialises in helping people manifest their hopes and wishes using intention practices and ceremony. Central to her work is *The Desire Pendant*, a powerful and exquisite piece of jewellery created for men and women. Dawn works with clients to help them understand and communicate what they desire to experience in life, and then infuses the chosen piece with their dreams.

For this activity I include two sets of instructions. The first option is a DIY intention job. Using a piece you already have, you will complete a ceremony presented by professional healer, Ellie Jackson. This process involves calling on benefic universal forces to help embed your intention into your piece and hold your vision. The second option involves engaging Dawn Wonder to supply your touchstone and infuse it with your vision. As part of this ceremony, she also personally holds your intention.

ACTIVITY 9

OPTION 1 – DIY INTENTION CEREMONY

The following ceremony instructions are provided by Ellie Jackson. Ideally, this clearing and intention ritual should be performed on the days either side of a full moon.

Required items:

- Pen or pencil
- *Workbook #2 Answer Sheet*
- Smudge stick made from white sage or a Palo Santo stick (can be purchased from a metaphysical store) and a white feather (optional)
- Ceramic bowl containing sand or dirt
- White clothing (not essential, but white does represent purity, clear intent and the light)
- White candle
- Compass (most smart phones have one)
- Music track (Ellie recommends playing Deva Premal's *Om the Cosmic Yes*)
- Your intention summary, created in *Activity 2*.

Step 1: Choose your touchstone

Do you already have a treasured object, one associated with fond memories? For me, a sacred object could include a heart-shaped rock found following the loss of a loved one or a beautiful seashell discovered in the desert when travelling. If you don't have a specific touchstone in mind, make a list of items that hold a special place in your heart, then contemplate and choose which one to use.

Step 2: Clearing negative energy from your yourself

Before working with your object, it is important to clean your own energy field by following these steps:

1. Begin with several minutes of heart-brain coherence. Then, hold the intention to remove any negative energy from your personal field. *Note: See* Activity 5, Step 3 *to revisit the instructions for creating heart-brain coherence.*

2. To cleanse your energy, you will use the white smoke emitted from a smudge stick (a bundle of white sage) or a stick of Palo Santo. Ideally, use a gas firelighter to ignite the sage or Palo Santo stick, rather than matches or a lighter. Hold the stick over the flame for approximately 30 seconds until it begins to smoke. Gently blow on the stick to help the ignition process, being careful of stray embers.

3. Move the smoking stick in figure-of-eight motions around your body. Start at your left foot and work your way up the leg, the left side of your body and your left arm (left signifies the past). Then work your way across your chest and down your right arm until you reach your right foot (right signifies the future).

4. Make your way up the front of your body along the central line, moving over your head and down the back of your body. You may find it is easier to work in tandem with someone else. When doing so, take turns in clearing each other. To help disperse the smoke, you may like to use a white feather. As you do so, imagine a beam of white light pouring down from above, filling up your entire body until it is aglow with light.

Step 3: Clearing negative energy from your object

Now that you have cleansed your energy field, you will need to remove any negative energy from your treasured object so that it is ready to be imbued with your vision. This will enhance its power.

1. Working again in figure-of-eight motions, cover all surfaces of the object with smoke. As you do so, imagine your object being filled with white light.

2. When you have finished clearing yourself and your object, extinguish the sage or Palo Santo stick by placing the ignited end into a ceramic bowl containing sand or dirt. Discard any ashes onto the ground outside, so the Earth can absorb and process the negative energy, being careful not to start a wildfire.

Step 4: Charge your object under the full moon

Now that your object is 'clean', you may wish to charge it under the potent energy of the full moon. Doing so will further amplify the power of your object, fuelling your intention. If this process is new to you, follow the steps below:

1. After sunset, place your object on the ground outside so that it is directly under the moonlight and can absorb maximal lunar energy overnight. Do so with the intent that your object will be used as a receptacle for your purpose-filled vision and will be charged with benefic universal forces.

2. If the area outside is not secure, you can leave your item indoors on a window ledge, preferably with the window open so that the moonbeams are not filtered through glass.

3. If it is a cloudy night and the moon is not visible, this practice will still be effective.

4. Collect your charged object in the morning with gratitude and thanks.

Step 5: Infuse your object with your vision

Set aside one hour of uninterrupted time, when you are feeling calm and in good spirits. Play *Om the Cosmic Yes* by Deva Premal, and keep it on repeat throughout the following ceremony to help hold the space and maintain the energy vibration:

1. Face the east, light a white candle and place your sacred object on the ground directly in front of it. Then clear your energy again, as described in *Step 2* above.

2. Make 'sacred space' by mentally drawing a circle of golden light on the ground around you. This energetic circle acts to protect and contain the energy of the ceremony.

3. Honour the four directions – east, south, west and north – and call in the guardians of each direction. This is done by reverently bowing first to the east (direction of new beginnings) and saying out loud, *I call in the Guardian of the East.* (This can also be done silently, but it is more powerful if said out loud.) Working clockwise, turn to the south and repeat the process. Once you have acknowledged all four directions and invited in the guardians, turn again to face the east and sit down.

4. Acknowledge the original custodians of the land and call their spirits into the circle. If possible, refer to them by name (you might be able to find this information online). Doing so is more respectful and as a result, your ceremony will be more powerful. You can use a statement like: *I honour the ancestors and the elders, past and present, and the spirits of the land.*

5. Call on your Spirit Guides who love you unconditionally. These benevolent forces, gathered into your circle, will hold

and help you attain your vision, providing it is for the highest good of all.

6. Close your eyes and breathe deeply in and out from your heart centre. Open your eyes and read your intention summary out loud to your benefic witnesses. As you do so, hold your vision in your mind's eye and embody the sensations of living your vision.

7. Close your eyes again and continue to envisage yourself joyfully living your vision while you chant the word *Om*, which is pronounced *ahh oooo mmm* and signifies the Universe's primordial energy. As you chant, imagine being immersed in a column of while light coming down from above and up from the ground, before rippling out from your heart centre in all directions (similar to a ripple created by a pebble). This practice sends your intention into your object, your surroundings and out into the Universe.

8. Sit in stillness for approximately five minutes while giving thanks to your guidance for your vision 'having been fulfilled'. Before you close the ceremony, ask the benefic forces present for any further guidance. Be open to receiving any messages that might come during the ceremony itself or in the following days, weeks and months. Acknowledge and give thanks for any messages received.

9. Finally, bring your awareness back into your body. Feel where your body connects to the earth. Wiggle your fingers and toes. Take a couple of deep breaths. Open your eyes.

10. Blow out the candle and relax in the knowledge that benefic universal forces with pure intent are holding your vision. Trust that it is in the process of being realised. Use your charged object as a constant reminder to align your thoughts, words, emotions and actions with your deepest desires.

OPTION 2 – INTENTION SERVICE

Step 1: Go shopping

Visit Dawn's *Wonder and Desire* website to select and purchase your *Desire Pendant:*

www.dawnwonder.com/the-pendant

The *Desire Pendant* is available in two sizes:

- Small – 22 mm
- Large – 30 mm.

The materials and metals available include:

- Sterling silver – with or without gemstone
- Sterling silver – with black enamel
- White gold – with diamond centre set (special order)
- Gold – with diamond centre set (special order).

Note: Website prices reflect pendant costs only. Feel free to wear the pendant on your favourite chain or contact Dawn to enquire about a special chain order.

Step 2: Book an Intention Session

An *Intention Session* is designed to help you create sacred intentions for your *Desire Pendant* and instruct you on how and when to use it as a touchstone.

When booking this session, you will need to provide Dawn with a short summary encapsulating your vision and/or any specific desires you wish to focus on as a priority. I recommend sending her the intention summary you created in *Activity 2.* Articulating your desires in this way will provide Dawn with the information she needs to perform the *Infusion Ceremony,* detailed below in *Step 3.*

Here is the URL to find out more and book your *Intention Session*:

www.dawnwonder.com/services

Step 3: **Book your Infusion Ceremony**

An *Infusion Ceremony* converts your *Desire Pendant* from an exquisite piece of jewellery into a powerful personal touchstone. During this sacred ceremony, Dawn holds the intention of your desires and charges them directly into your *Desire Pendant*.

To find out more and book your *Infusion Ceremony* visit:

www.dawnwonder.com/services

Once the ceremony is complete, your *Desire Pendant* will be shipped to you.

Step 4: **Cherish your Desire Pendant**

When your *Desire Pendant* arrives, set aside some time to unwrap this special piece and become acquainted with it. Wear your pendant as a constant reminder to align your thoughts, words, emotions and actions with your deepest desires. Also, relax in the knowledge that someone who has no emotional attachment to the outcome is holding your vision and trust that it is in the process of being realised.

REHEARSAL SCHEDULE

Now that you have completed the activities, you should have a powerful and tangible heart-centred life vision that reflects your aspirations, deepest desires, tastes, passions and, above all, your life's purpose.

Completing the activities, however, is not a one-off. If your vision is to reach fruition, it needs to be at the forefront of your mind. Repeatedly and consistently simulating the experience of living your desired future embeds it at a subconscious level. When your subconscious mind accepts this reality as truth, your outer world moulds itself to match your inner experience.

For your convenience I've created a daily-weekly-monthly rehearsal schedule that is based on the activities you've just completed with a few additional tips. Ideally, you would adhere to each of the practices listed. If things get stale at any stage, take a break or mix things up. The envisioning work should never feel like a chore. It's meant to be fun and inspiring. If you are doing it correctly, it will feel like an escape from your current reality.

Daily

Upon waking

The following actions will help set your mood for the day:

- Play your mind movie the moment you wake (*Activity 5, Steps 1–5*).

- Listen to inspiring and uplifting content over a cup of tea, during breakfast, while you are getting ready to leave the house, or on your way to work.

During your day

- Envision a favourite scene from your mind movie, particularly at peak times of stress (*Activity 5, Step 6*).

- Play your vision soundtrack and/or music that affirms you having fulfilled your vision (such as *Mind Songs*) throughout your day (*Activity 3*). If the situation allows, let loose and dance/move to the music. This helps to create a feeling of well-being and pleasurable sensations throughout your entire body, prompting elevated emotions.

- Read and/or listen to inspiring content. Wherever possible, refrain from consuming content that conveys negative messaging, whether that be via social media, music, radio, television and so on.

- Wear or carry your touchstone throughout the day as a prompt to align your thoughts, words, emotions and actions with your deepest desires. Handle it whenever you need reassurance that your current reality is only temporary and that your vision is in the process of being realised (*Activity 9*).

- At opportune moments, such as waiting for a friend, riding on public transport, walking to work or standing in line at the grocery store, envision what it would feel like to be your future self. Consciously embody the associated characteristics and traits, such as postures, behaviours and thoughts (*Activity 6*).

Before bed

As mentioned earlier, your subconscious mind is more easily influenced just before falling asleep, making it important to have an evening routine as well.

- Play your mind movie one hour prior to bed (*Activity 5, Steps 1–5*). *Note: Do not look at any LED devices such as a computer, phone or television within one hour of bed as the blue light they emit may impact your ability to fall asleep. Similarly, don't look at LED screens in the middle of the night.*

- Spend a few minutes journaling about all the things you are grateful for and recap on the highlights from your day. Jot down any positive incidents and fortuitous events that occurred, such as a scenario you'd dreaded that turned out for the best or an unexpected financial gain. This could be as minor as being treated to lunch by a friend. Keep a running journal to track the positive changes in your life and the events that unfold in alignment with your vision.

- Immediately prior to switching off the light, take a moment to read your intention summary (created in *Activity 2, Step 2*). *Note: Ensure you read a paper copy rather than one stored on an electrical device, as advised above.* How you feel just prior to bed impacts your sleep, dreams and how you wake up of a morning.

Weekly

- Take the time to create screen savers, regularly 'pin' images and decorate your surroundings with elements that depict your vision. This type of subliminal messaging serves as a constant reminder to the subconscious mind.

- Read your 'ideal day' creative narrative (*Activity 2, Step 1*).

- Review your week. If you've been journaling every day, you might like to reflect on your notes. Observe any recurring patterns or themes – positive and negative. For negative experiences, identify any causative beliefs and apply your PSYCH-K® skills to check and balance them (*Activity 7, Step 3*).

- Participate in Lynne McTaggart's Intention of the Week. This is a self-directed exercise performed from 10 am to 10.30 am every Sunday, Pacific USA time. To learn more, visit:

  www.lynnemctaggart.com/intention-experiments/intentions-of-the-week/

- Meet and intend with your Power of Eight group (*Activity 8, Steps 2–5*).

Monthly

Review your progress by asking yourself the following questions:

- Have I been able to stick with the daily/weekly schedule?
- Do I still feel inspired by my vision?
- Do I find mental rehearsal and role play fun and uplifting?
- Am I beginning to see some positive changes in my outer world?

If you answered *no* to any of these questions, you might need to do some belief-change balances around any resistance to doing the work (*Activity 7, Step* 3). Alternatively, take a break for a few days or revisit your vision and tweak it slightly (repeat *Activities 1–4*). It could be as simple as reviewing your list from *Activity 1* and writing a new scene into your creative narrative (*Activity 2*) or building another movie that incorporates different elements from your ideal day (*Activity 4*). Having a selection of mind movies that encapsulate your vision will help keep your practice fresh and on theme.

Note: Repetition is important for neurologically becoming your future self, so don't mix things up too much until you've been doing the envisioning work for a couple of months.

CONCLUSION

Congratulations! You have begun bridging the gap between your current reality and the life you truly desire. By repeatedly 'experiencing' your dream future, you will have gained the sense of how much happier you will be living that life, as well as the confidence to embrace new opportunities and restructure your life.

If this is where you find yourself, it can be very tempting to rush out and begin making sweeping changes to produce the life you've been rehearsing, mentally and physically. A word of caution before you race down that path. I've made changes hastily in the past without doing further 'inner work' and it didn't end well.

I encourage you to work methodically through the remainder of my workbook series. The reason? At this stage of our journey together, you have created and reinforced neural pathways that support your vision and established strong foundations for freely expressing yourself across all aspects of life. However, there are significant physical actions and emotional changes required for your vision to become a lived reality, and the framework I provide in the subsequent workbooks sets you up for positive experiences rather than painful ones.

In *Workbook #3* I step you through a complete audit of your life to eliminate the things that no longer serve you and make room for the 'new'. This part of the journey tends to stir up suppressed and deep-seated emotions that must be processed and released prior to continuing. Without this stage you will find yourself building on unstable foundations and all your hard work is likely to collapse, potentially causing further wounding and keeping you trapped in your old patterns.

Physically and emotionally spring cleaning your life acts to permanently raise your emotional baseline. Operating at this new, elevated state enhances the effectiveness of your mental rehearsal and role play because you are now more energetically and physically aligned with your emotionally charged vision. This inner shift further strengthens your power to draw in the life you desire, and the results become almost unbelievable.

Synchronicities and meaningful coincidences become a way of life. Doors that were closed suddenly open and pathways that didn't exist unexpectedly appear. I've personally experienced such phenomena countless times. I've been the beneficiary of jaw-dropping events, circumstances and opportunities that even the best event or project manager could not have orchestrated (but that's a story for another time). That is the intention I hold for you.

Personalised support

Be aware that the journey of self-discovery and the process of change can often be difficult and isolating, particularly when there is an enormous gap between where you are now and where you desire to be. I found it essential to have someone whom I trusted and could turn to when the going got tough. A mentor who understood the journey I was on and could give me clarity and personalised advice.

You don't have to go it alone. I offer one-on-one *Personalised Guidance* sessions if you have questions about the workbook content or need further support on your journey.

To book a session, simply email:
kylie@aguideforlife.com

Developing your tool kit

I strongly advise that you build a tool kit to support you on this journey. Following are some ideas.

Books

As you complete the *Workbook Series* curriculum, you will acquire a library of written resources. I encourage you to read these books from start to finish, at a later stage. Doing so will enhance your appreciation of the journey and reinforce your understanding of how to successfully build a life you love. Most importantly these resources will help you comprehend just how powerful you are and unlock your unfulfilled potential, so you can be a full expression of your magnificent, uninhibited self. The *Inspirational Resources* section also provides further recommended reading.

Audio

Consistently immersing yourself in self-help audio resources will help you transition from your current reality to one in which you can freely express yourself. I've found having something inspirational to listen to as I'm waking up with my first cup of tea sets my mood for the day. It also puts me to sleep of an evening and settles me down quickly if I'm having trouble going back to sleep in the middle of the night.

I suggest you choose audio books in line with the principles in the *Build a Life You Love Workbook Series*. You may also benefit from lectures and interviews featuring those who have successfully navigated the journey you are on. You'll find plenty of recommendations to get you started in the *Inspirational Resources* section. Happy listening!

Power tools

Throughout the *Build a Life You Love Workbook Series*, I recommend modalities and processes to help facilitate change, in both yourself and others. They are highly effective and simple to learn. I like to think of these as 'power tools' for changing your reality. I promise that they will come in handy if you find yourself having a meltdown in the middle of the night or your regular practitioner has a waiting list days-weeks-months long. Having these tools at your disposal will save you a small fortune in the long run.

I also recommend DIY practices and rituals to help you manage your emotions (particularly your fears) and support you in overcoming self-limiting mindsets and self-destructive behaviours when making major edits to your life.

I wish you well on your journey of self-discovery. It is the most gratifying and meaningful adventure you could ever embark on! Enjoy every moment and be as present as possible, regardless of the challenges you encounter. Trust your intuition. Take notice of the things that catch your attention, arouse your curiosity and evoke excitement.

My hope is that by sharing the resources and tools I found to be the most effective, your path from hereon will be smoother and more direct. May you live a joyful and fulfilling life that is also meaningful, making the world a better place.

Here's to living your ultimate future.

With love,

Kylie Xo

Kylie Attwell
www.aguideforlife.com

APPENDIX 1:
CREATE A VISION BOARD

If you are more 'old school' and would prefer to create a physical representation of the person you aspire to be and the life you desire to live, you could make a vision board.

Required resources

- Magazines and catalogues you don't mind cutting up, copies of favourite photos and/or inspiring images you've found online
- Scissors or another cutting implement
- Blank canvas, or a sheet of ply, MDF or thick cardboard
- Symbolic decorative items such as hearts, stars, glitter, stickers (a craft or scrapbooking shop will have a huge range)
- Glue or adhesive that is suitable for the chosen materials
- Future fragrance
- Background music that evokes a sense of inner peace and focus.

Instructions

1. When gathering images, choose pictures that inspire you, reflect who you are and represent the life you desire. If you can't find exactly the right images, select those that symbolise your personal goals. For example, if you desire to live in a house by the beach but can't find the perfect picture, then you might like to include an image of rolling surf to represent the view from your dream home.

2. Selecting your final images is an intuitive process that should be done quickly. Don't spend hours poring over and contemplating each image. Instead, choose colours

that you are drawn to and images that catch your eye and immediately speak to your heart.

3. Trim your images to the desired shape and arrange them in a format that is visually pleasing. Some people prefer not to overlap their images, arranging them neatly so that they fit together in a symmetrical pattern with clearly defined borders around each image. Others like their collage to be less structured, layering and haphazardly positioning their images. You might even decide to lay out your images in a particular shape such as a heart, star or oval.

4. Add motivational affirmations or words that represent how you want to feel such as *joyful, abundant, powerful, fearless, loved, strong, healthy, loving* and *financially free*. You can write the words on coloured paper or directly onto the board. You could also cut words or letters from magazines. If pressed for time, you could type out the phrases and words, and then print them. That way you'll have an endless array of fonts, colours and sizes to choose from. Alternatively, you might like to use a label maker. *Note: If you require assistance with writing affirmations, detailed instructions are provided in* Appendix 3.

5. Once you are satisfied with the layout, glue the images and text into position.

6. Put your vision board somewhere prominent. Look at it for a couple of minutes every day and envisage achieving your goals and living the life it depicts.

7. As your dreams begin to manifest, your vision board becomes evidence that the process is working. Make sure you celebrate every success.

APPENDIX 2:
MIND MOVIES 4.0 CREATION KIT INSTRUCTIONS

Images

Below are the instructions for viewing and uploading images to your movie:

Mind Movies stock images

1. Select the 'Pictures' tab to open the 'Mind Movies Library'. The stock material in the library is arranged into different categories to aid in finding the perfect image for your movie; for example, *Friends & Family, House/Apartment, Relationships.*

2. Peruse the image categories listed on the left of the screen and click on the one you would like to browse, such as *Exercise.*

3. Exercise-related images will then load. Scroll through them by clicking on the page numbers just below the images.

4. To take a closer look at one of the thumbnail pictures in the library, click on it and a larger preview will open. To close the image and continue browsing, click 'X' in the top right-hand corner of the image.

5. To add an image to your mind movie, click on the one you want to use, drag it down into the blue timeline section below and release the image by unclicking it.

6. Insert enough imagery (30 to 45 images) to make your mind movie run for 2 to 3 minutes. To determine the length of your mind movie, hold the cursor over the last image you uploaded, and the total time will be displayed.

7. There are two ways to adjust how long an image appears on the screen:

i. Hover over the bottom left corner of the frame until a box with the number two appears (i.e. the default is set to 2 seconds) and then type in your desired duration.

ii. Click on the blue 'lines' icon located in the bottom right-hand corner of each frame and slide the purple toggle up or down to increase or decrease the image duration as desired. *Note: Within this mode, you can also adjust affirmation duration and transition zoom/rotate features, as detailed below.*

Upload your own images

I. Select the 'Pictures' tab in *Mind Movies* and click on 'More Actions'.

2. Click on 'Upload My Own Pictures' from the dropdown menu.

3. Either select 'Choose Files' and select an image from a folder on your computer or drag and drop images straight from your desktop or photo application onto the *Mind Movies* screen. The images will then begin to upload. You can also upload images from Facebook by clicking on 'Import from Facebook'. To do this you will first need to log in to your Facebook account.

4. When the image has been uploaded, it will be stored in the 'My Library' section and can be accessed from there to add an image to your mind movie.

Reordering images

1. To rearrange the order of images, click on the one you wish to move and drag it to the desired position.

2. To add additional images, simply click on the double-headed arrow marked 'Insert' between frames.

Videos

Mind Movies has a small library of videos that will help to animate your movie, or you can import and use your own. When using your own videos, you will need to upload them to YouTube first. If you need assistance setting up your own YouTube account, search the phrase 'Create an account on YouTube' to find a video that instructions you on the process.

Below are the instructions for adding videos to your mind movie:

Mind Movies stock videos

1. Select the 'Video' tab in *Mind Movies*.

2. Peruse the categories and add the chosen video/s to your mind movie as per the instructions for adding stock images outlined above.

3. Next, you'll be asked to adjust the length of time you want the video to play. The default is 4 seconds, which is generally suitable. If you'd like to change this, simply slide the purple toggle up or down to increase or decrease the image duration as desired. Alternatively, you can type the number of seconds in the white box. When complete click 'Continue'.

4. Insert enough imagery to make your mind movie run for 2 to 3 minutes.

Upload your own videos

Note: To use this function you need to have your own video library on YouTube.

1. Select the 'Videos' tab in *Mind Movies* and click on 'Insert YouTube Video Clip'.

2. When the next screen opens, drag the red YouTube icon on to the timeline where you would like the video to appear.

3. A window with 'Insert YouTube Video' will appear on the screen.

4. Log in to your YouTube account and find the video you would like to use. Copy and paste the URL into the area provided and click on 'Get Movie'.

5. You can choose to play the entire video or just a portion. To play the entire video adjust the red sliding bar underneath the video so that it fills the whole timeframe. If you would like to select a portion of the video, for example from the 10–25 second mark, start the red bar at the 00:00:10 and end it at the 00:00:25.

6. You can also choose to play the sound from your YouTube video clip or the soundtrack from your mind movie. Select either 'The Sound from the Video Clip' or 'The Music you selected for the Mind Movie' options.

7. Once you've made your selections click on 'Insert Clip'.

Reordering videos

1. To rearrange the order of videos, click on the one you wish to move and drag it to the desired position.

2. To add additional videos, simply click on the double-headed arrow marked 'Insert' between frames.

Affirmations

Adding affirmations from the *Mind Movies* library is similar to choosing imagery.

Choose your affirmations

1. Select the 'Affirmations' tab in *Mind Movies* and click on the categories of interest.

2. Click on your chosen affirmation drag it onto the image you want to pair it with in the blue timeline section. *Note: The appearance of the affirmation can be customised, as detailed below.*

If you prefer to write your own affirmations, you can do so using the following instructions.

Add your own affirmations

An affirmation should have certain attributes to maximise its effectiveness. If you require assistance with crafting your affirmations, detailed instructions are provided in *Appendix 3*. Once you have created your affirmation, take the following steps in *Mind Movies*:

1. Select the image or video you would like to write an affirmation for and click on the 'Customise Text'.

2. Type your affirmation into the 'Insert Custom Text' in the window that opens. *Note: The appearance of the affirmation can be customised, as outlined below.*

3. Once you have finished writing the affirmation, click on 'Save'.

Customise affirmation appearance

You can customise the affirmation appearance by adjusting the font format and style. You can also change the position of your affirmation, its duration and the way it appears on the screen.

1. Select the image or video frame that contains the affirmation you would like to edit and then click on 'Customise Text'.

2. Adjust the font format and style by choosing from various options at the top of the window, such as font type, size, bold, italics, underlining and colour.

3. Choose the position of the affirmation in the window by selecting options in the bottom left of the window.

4. You can also adjust image and text duration and choose how the text transitions on to the image.

5. Once you have finished personalising the appearance of your affirmations, click on 'Save'.

Special/visual effects

Adding special effects to the way images and videos appear will not impact the effectiveness of your mind movie. It comes down to personal taste. If you feel this is something that will enhance the production of your movie, follow the steps below.

When uploading your movie imagery, you may have noticed a vertically positioned rectangular object (with a word written on it) between the frames. These vertical objects carry the transition information affecting how one image or video transitions to the next, and this can be customised. *Note: It is not possible to delete transitions altogether.*

1. To customise the way one image or video transitions to another, select the 'Transitions' tab in *Mind Movies* and choose the category you would like to explore.

2. To see the transition effects, click on one of the parrot images.

3. To add a transition to your mind movie, click on it and drag it down onto the vertical rectangular object positioned between the frames of the transition you wish to modify.

4. If you wish to disable the zoom/rotate feature, click on the blue 'lines' icon located in the bottom right-hand corner of each frame, and select the features you wish to disable. Using this function, you can also adjust how long an image and affirmation appears for on the screen (the default is 2 seconds).

Soundtrack

As mentioned earlier, the soundtrack of your mind movie is extremely important. You can choose one from the *Mind Movies* library or import your own music.

Mind Movies soundtracks

1. Select the 'Music' tab in *Mind Movies* to peruse the extensive catalogue.

2. Click on any song to hear a sample.

3. When you have found one you like, select 'Apply' to add it to your movie.

Upload your own music

If you have composed your own music or you are legally authorised to use an audio track created by someone else (such as Amorita, mentioned in *Activity 3)*, you can add it to your movie. *Note: You cannot add any commercial music to your mind movie unless you have permission from the relevant copyright collecting society.*

Below are the instructions for uploading your own music:

1. Select the 'Music' tab.

2. Click on 'More Action' and choose 'Upload My Own Music' from the dropdown menu.

3. Select 'Browse' and select the file you wish to upload from your desktop.

4. Check the 'I am legally authorised to use this audio' box.

5. Give the audio track a title and click on 'Submit'.

6. When the audio file has been uploaded, it will be stored in the 'My Library' section. To access this track simply click on 'My Library', located next to 'Mind Movies Library'.

7. To add this track to your movie, click on it and hit 'Apply'.

Subliminal audio

Below are the instructions for adding subliminal audio to your soundtrack:

1. Select the 'Music' tab in *Mind Movies*.

2. Click on 'More Actions' and choose 'Add Subliminal Audio' from the dropdown menu.

3. Peruse the subliminal audio tracks and choose one that matches the theme of your mind movie.

4. A '✓' will appear next to the track you have selected, click 'Apply'.

Review, save, process and download movie

Now that you have put together your movie it's time to review it.

1. Click on 'Step 2 Preview', located underneath the blue timeline section to play your movie.

2. When finished click the 'X' in the corner to close that window.

3. Make any changes or adjustments by repeating *Steps 1–7* in *Activity 4*.

4. When you are happy with your movie, click 'Step 3 Save Project', located underneath the blue timeline section.

5. Give your video a title and a description, then hit 'Save'.

6. Click 'Step 4 Send to Processor', located underneath the blue timeline section.

7. A window will open asking you if you want to publish your mind movie on Facebook or YouTube. *Note: This is optional. It is not necessary for you to share your mind movie for it to be processed.* If you click 'Yes' to these options, you must be logged into your Facebook or YouTube account in another browser window.

8. Click 'Send to Processor'. *Note: Processing your movie can take some time. When processing is complete, you will receive an email letting you know that your video is ready.*

Downloading to your computer

1. To view your mind movie, click on the 'My Videos' window in *Mind Movies*.

2. You will be given the option to download or share your movie. To download it to your Mac, select 'Download Video'. If you are using a PC, select 'Windows Video'.

3. Your movie will then download onto your computer. The file will download as a .mov on Mac and .wmv on a PC.

Downloading to iPhone/iPad/Android from app

1. Download the *Mind Movies app* to your smart device via the App Store on your Apple device or Google Play if you use an Android.

2. Open the app and log into your *Mind Movies* account.

3. Select your movie, then choose from 'Watch Now', 'Watch Later' or 'Download to Watch Offline'.

4. By selecting 'Watch Now' you can watch your movie within the app.

5. If you'd like to download your movie to your smart device so you can watch it whenever and wherever you are, select the 'Download to Watch Offline' option.

6. 'Creation Kit' will then ask to access your Photos app. Hit 'Select'.

7. You'll then be prompted to open the Photos app, where the video is stored.

8. Select your movie and press the 'Play' icon.

Downloading to iTunes/iPhone/iPad/iPod without app

If you do not wish to download the *Mind Movies* app onto your device, you will need to add your movie to your iTunes account.

1. Open up 'Movies' within the iTunes Library on your computer, then drag and drop your movie into the iTunes Movie Library.

2. Connect your device to your computer and click on 'iPhone/iPad/iPod' in the iTunes menu.

3. Select the 'Movies' tab and then 'Sync Movies' box.

4. '✓' your movie title and click on 'Sync'.

5. Once synchronisation is complete, your movie will appear in the iMovie app on your Apple device.

6. Select your movie and press the 'Play' icon.

Downloading to Android without app

You can add a mind movie to your Android smartphone in two different ways:

1. Download your movie to your computer, connect your phone to your computer and transfer the movie to your smartphone.

2. Log in to your *Mind Movies* account on your smartphone (you need to be connected to the internet on your phone) and download your movie directly to your smartphone using the Windows Video option underneath the video in the downloads option.

APPENDIX 3:
INSTRUCTIONS FOR WRITING AFFIRMATIONS

An affirmation is a statement that declares something to be true. In the context of manifesting your desires, there are a few rules that make affirmations more powerful:

- The first and most fundamental attribute of an affirmation is its truth to you. The reason? The mind creates resistance to affirmations that are not true in that moment. It was prosperity teacher Marilyn Jenett who confirmed this principle for me. She suggests that instead of using statements such as *I am wealthy*, when you are struggling to pay your bills and feed yourself, you might use *I am now ready to increase my income*, or *My finances improve every day*, or *I am ready to own my own home*.

  Similarly, if you are single, instead of using *My partner and I are perfectly aligned*, you might start with *I am now ready to meet my divine life partner*. If you are wishing to lose weight, rather than *My body is fit and healthy*, a phrase such as *I am now ready to achieve my ideal body weight* or *My body craves food that is healthy for me* might resonate with you and feel more truthful.

- Always write in first person (e.g. *I, me, my*) and where possible, start with a powerful statement such as *I am*.

- Use present tense. Do not use phrases that reference dates or time, such as *future* or *two months from now*.

- Create simple power statements of already having your desire. Do not use phrases that include *I want* or *I need*. Do not get caught up in describing the how.

- Affirmations must be stated positively.

- Be specific. Do not use phrases that state what you don't want. Instead, determine what you do want, and then create statements that describe what you desire to have or experience.

- Don't use words that have negative connotations such as *cancer*, *illness*, *disease*, *smoking*, *poisonous* or *toxins*.

- Make them short and sweet. Statements that are concise and to the point are more powerful. Below are some examples of short statements incorporating the above principles:

  - *I am a radiant being filled with vitality and energy.*
  - *I am worthy of receiving abundance.*
  - *My partner treats me with love and respect.*
  - *Every day and in every way I am getting better and better.*
  - *Opportunities open up easily and effortlessly for me.*

- Finally, be emotive. Use phrases that convey passion and feeling, such as:

  - *I enjoy improving the life of others.*
  - *I give thanks for my radiant health and happiness.*
  - *I am happy and grateful that...*
  - *I choose to be kind.*
  - *I accept others for who they are.*
  - *I deeply appreciate my...*
  - *I expect...*
  - *I easily attract...*

If you would like further affirmation inspiration, you could explore the work of Florence Scovel Shinn or Louise Hay, both pioneers in this area.

APPENDIX 4:
'ACT AS IF' EVENT PLAN

TWO MONTHS BEFORE (MINIMUM)

☐ **Who will you be in five years?**

Consider who you would like to be in five years. What will your accomplishments be and what will it feel like to achieve these goals?

_____

_____

_____

_____

_____

_____

_____

_____

☐ **Determine your budget and party type**

Throwing a party can get rather costly very quickly, so you may prefer to host an intimate dinner instead. This can be just as effective, if not more so, because you and your dinner guests will need to hold a conversation in character within a small group for a few hours. This can be far more challenging than mingling with a large crowd and conversing with others for only a few minutes at a time.

If your heart is set on throwing a gala event, you may well be able to pull off a lavish affair on a shoestring budget using creativity, ingenuity and a little help from your friends. For instance, you could engage: unemployed actors or drama students to play the paparazzi and adoring fans; budding rock stars or a friend with an awesome music collection for the entertainment; a foodie nut or fledging chef to feed the hoards; and an event management student to make your party one to remember. In this way you can stretch your budget to hold a more grandiose event, with the added bonus of helping your recruits role-play their aspirations.

If money is not an issue, you could go wild recreating Jack Canfield's party examples. Alternatively, you may have your own creative ideas for a role-play gathering that more closely suits your circumstances. I encourage you to do what feels right.

Practical considerations

For inspiration on how to bring your event to life, research Pinterest, blogs and magazines for dramatization ideas.

☐ Organise a venue

Hosting your event at home can save you a lot of money, but considering another location might enhance your 'act as if' experience. For example, your home might hold memories that prevent you seeing a new future, while an opulent restaurant or the spectacular views at a friend's home might provide a better backdrop to celebrate your success. If you decide to throw a gala event, it's best to find a suitable venue and confirm its availability prior to fixing the date.

Practical considerations

When hiring a venue, make sure you are aware of all the costs involved and what the hire agreement does and doesn't include to ensure nothing limits or dampens the effectiveness of your celebratory event. Be aware of the following:

- A short event duration can be limiting. Your party will need to wrap up at a prescribed time, rather than allowing it to organically end when guests are ready to say their goodbyes.

- Although most of the clean-up will be taken care of with a hired venue, you will still need to oversee and ensure all party equipment and goods have been packed up and removed when handing the venue back. It might a good idea to assign this role to someone else.

- Some venues are flexible with their event packages while others require you to use in-house services only (e.g. food and beverage, audio and visual equipment). Consider your event needs carefully as you may prefer to bring in an external caterer and/or AV supplier.

☐ Plan your guest list

Consider who you would like to invite. I suggest choosing those friends, family, acquaintances and colleagues who relish fancy dress parties and will go all out in terms of dressing the part and staying in character throughout.

Practical considerations

With a gala event the expected turnout is usually around 70–80%. Factor this in when planning catering, entertainment, venue size and so on.

_____

_____

_____

_____

_____

_____

_____

_____

_____

_____

_____

_____

_____

_____

_____

☐ Confirm a date and time

Select the event date at least a month or two in advance. This gives guests enough time to consider how they would like to portray their ideal self, including attire and props. I also recommend choosing a date that falls on a weekend, so they have enough time to get into costume and character, instead of rushing to your event straight from work. Make sure you have no other major priorities on or around the date you have chosen.

Practical considerations

Before settling on a day, you might like to send out a 'save the date' memo to ensure key guests are available to attend.

_____

_____

_____

_____

_____

_____

☐ Invite your guests

Determine whether you are going to send paper or e-invitations. Although more costly, paper invitations can act as a tangible visual reminder for guests to RSVP and turn up to the event.

The invitation should include the *date, time, location, RSVP cut off* and *intent* of your party. Most importantly you need to clearly communicate the event objective of 'celebrating your dreams having come true'. It's essential that guests are instructed to speak only in present tense for the entire event, as if they have already achieved their goals and fulfilled their dreams. Also suggest ways in which guests can stay in character throughout the party, including what to wear, how to behave, and props that could add a level of reality to their performance and that of others.

In addition to paper invitations, you could also create a special event page on social media, such as Facebook. This may help to inspire and excite guests about your party while hopefully maximising turnout.

Practical considerations

If you are still unsure of wording, you might like to closely model your invitation on the 'come as you will be in five years from now party' in *The Success Principles*.

_____

_____

_____

_____

_____

_____

_____

_____

_____

_____

_____

_____

_____

_____

_____

☐ Book entertainment and extras

Ideally, you would capture this event on film to share later with your guests as a tangible daily reminder of their future. If you are going all out, I encourage you to hire a professional photographer and/or videographer. For a small dinner party, you can set up a video camera discretely in the corner. Photo booths are another fun way to capture memories from the event. For some reason, people are often less inhibited when let loose in a photo booth.

Music, lighting and styling are also important factors for the success of an event. Music will fuel the atmosphere, whether provided by a band, DJ or a playlist you create for the event. Lighting can transform a venue, setting the tone or mood you want to achieve. If you have the budget, consider hiring an event stylist to direct of your event and create a cohesive look and feel. This may include colour palette, mood lighting, signage, furniture selection and floor plan, table setting, decorations and flowers – right down to the most intricate embellishments. It is the styling details that make your event memorable and special. If you choose to take on this role yourself, keep it simple. Less is always more.

You might like to enlist a few friends to help on the day. For example, some of your shy friends may love to participate by lending a hand, but dressing up may not be their thing.

Practical considerations

If applicable, be sure the venue manager knows all your plans and details in advance. Find out who your go-to staff will be and form a relationship with them early on.

☐ Organise catering

Make sure you consider guests' needs and the style of event. For example, do your guests have allergies or special dietary requirements? If hosting a cocktail-style event, you will need to serve food that guests can easily eat while standing.

If you are using external caterers, ensure their availability and terms before confirming the date. Advise them of any important details and dietary considerations before they begin proposing a menu.

If you are taking charge of the cooking, devise a menu that is easy to prepare, preferably ahead of time, and that accommodates all guests.

Practical considerations

Ensure you communicate your choice of catering to guests. For example, if you are only serving hors d'oeuvres during dinner time, your guests might like to have a light meal before the event.

☐ **Character preparation**

To help remain in character throughout the event you might like to create a short narrative and rehearse it in your mind well before the day. Things to consider include:

- who you are
- what you have accomplished
- what it felt like to achieve this goal
- the major steps and milestones
- how this has improved your life or the world.

ONE MONTH BEFORE

☐ **Devise a program**

Create a run sheet outlining the order of proceedings for your event. This will give you and your event crew a general outline of timing and how the party will progress.

☐ Social media hype

Continue to ramp up your social media by sharing a weekly teaser leading up to the event.

_____

_____

_____

_____

_____

_____

_____

_____

☐ Organise your costume and props

Now that you have taken care of the major event details and coordination, it's time to start organising what you will wear. Choose clothes and props that communicate to yourself and others that you have achieved your goals and desires.

_____

_____

_____

_____

_____

_____

_____

☐ Place orders

Now you have locked in a venue, entertainment and catering, it's time to organise the finer details as applicable. These could include your costume, props (e.g. certificate, medal, book cover, press articles, photos), photographer, photo-booth, flowers, furniture and so on.

☐ Create a seating plan

If you are throwing a dinner party or seated gala, I advise not seating guests together if they know each other. The reason? It's very easy for couples and close friends to 'fall out of character' and revert to their usual banter, particularly if they haven't seen each other for some time. Also, most people tend to be less self-conscious when role-playing with a stranger than with someone who knows them well.

☐ **RSVP reminder**

Send a reminder to guests a few days before the RSVP due date. Then call or email guests who do not respond.

_____

_____

_____

_____

ONE WEEK BEFORE

☐ **Finalise event numbers**

Send a 'can't wait to see you' message to your guests approximately one week before your event. This will flush out those who are no longer able to attend. Confirm final numbers and any dietary updates with the caterer, if necessary.

_____

_____

_____

_____

_____

_____

_____

_____

☐ Finish DIY projects

Finish building any props or making decorations early in the week.

_____

_____

_____

_____

_____

_____

_____

_____

☐ Catering

If self-catering, take care of any preparation in the week leading up to the event, so there is less to do on the day.

_____

_____

_____

_____

_____

_____

_____

_____

_____

_____

DAY OF EVENT

☐ **Send reminder message**

Message your guests on the morning of the party to remind them of the event details, so they don't have to go hunting around for their invitation. You might also provide them with any last-minute hints, reminders and weather updates.

If you are in touch with your guests on social media, create some excitement with event teasers. Doing so will encourage them to bring their best attitude.

_____

_____

_____

_____

_____

_____

☐ **Venue set-up**

Don't leave venue set-up and decoration of your event until the last minute, whether it's in your own home or at a venue. You want to leave plenty of time to get yourself ready and in character. After all, that's the aim of this whole activity.

_____

_____

_____

_____

_____

_____

☐ Enjoy!

Once everything is in place and guests have arrived, stressing about details and issues that arise during the event will dampen the experience for you and everyone else. Above all, make sure you enjoy every moment of your future life.

AFTER THE PARTY

Be sure to thank the venue staff, helpers and guests. You can keep the party going by uploading photos and footage to any social media channels used to share information about the event. I suggest you invite guests to recap on any highlights and outcomes from the event.

BUILD A LIFE YOU LOVE WORKBOOKS 1–7

Imagineer Your Ultimate Future is second in the series of seven *Build a Life You Love* workbooks designed to help you create a life where you are free to express yourself fully. The topics covered in this series include the following:

Workbook #1 – Find Your Purpose, Change Your Life

- The key to living a fulfilling, meaningful and joyous life
- The importance of developing an intimate relationship with yourself and how to do so
- The difference between purpose and passion
- The steps to take and the questions to ask yourself to uncover the themes of your life purpose.

Workbook #2 – Imagineer Your Ultimate Future

- Why it's important to create an inspiring vision for your life that reflects your purpose and expresses who you really are
- The role thoughts and emotions play in manifesting your dreams
- How to create a clear and exciting vision that feels tangible and real
- How to activate your vision and change your brain neurologically to match your desired new life.

Workbook #3

- Why it's essential to clean up your life prior to taking any physical steps towards living your life purpose

- How to identify and eliminate aspects of your life that no longer serve you

- How to quickly and painlessly process the emotions that arise, particularly fear, guilt and deep sadness, as you start to leave the toxic people and aspects of your life behind.

Workbook #4

- The role your passions play in your daily life

- Resources for uncovering and expressing your passions.

Workbook #5

- The mind-body connection, the relationship between the brain and the mind, and the role the conscious and subconscious minds play in making your dreams a reality

- Why your day-to-day reality is simply a reflection of the story you have created about life, rather than what is true and indeed possible

- Why certain types of unwanted experiences recur in your life, despite your efforts to change romantic partners, get a new job or move to a new location

- How the thinking-feeling-feeling-thinking cycle makes changing unwanted habits and self-destructive behaviour so difficult

- The power of the subconscious mind and the ways in which it can be quickly and effectively reprogrammed, so you can change your reality and experience the life you truly desire

- Recommended tools and techniques that will interrupt your habit of spiralling into negativity and depression

- An effective four-pronged approach for establishing a new mindset, letting go of your emotional baggage, creating a shift in your perception of life and adopting new functional patterns of behaviour.

Workbook #6

- Exploration of the notion that life is gently guiding, directing and communicating with you at all times, warning you not to take a particular direction or that the timing isn't quite right

- How to recognise and interpret the synchronicities, meaningful coincidences, messages and signs that life is sending you.

Workbook #7

- Why trying to control situations or the future, attempting to make something happen in your life or forcing an outcome actually pushes what you want further away

- Effective techniques to help you surrender control, detach from the outcome and finally let go, so that the things you desire can begin to flow into your life.

If you would like to be advised of when the next workbook in the series is released, please feel free to register your interest by emailing:

kylie@aguideforlife.com
Please use the subject heading 'Workbook Series'.

You will be contacted as soon as the latest workbook is published.

INSPIRATIONAL RESOURCES

In this section, you will find invaluable resources for understanding the following:

- Why creating a vision for your life is crucial
- The role thoughts, feelings, beliefs and actions play in the manifestation process
- How to build a real, tangible and achievable vision
- Effective ways to activate your vision, thereby generating new neural pathways to become your desired self at a physiological level.

These resources will also assist you in discovering even more about yourself and provide you with examples of everyday people and historic icons *who realised their vision.* In saying that, I recommend you keep it simple for now and only explore these resources when instructed to do so or when you've finished working your way through the entire workbook.

RECOMMENDED READING

- *Becoming Supernatural: How Common People Are Doing the Uncommon* by Dr Joe Dispenza. (Hay House Inc. 2019) Available in print and Kindle.

What if you could train your brain to tune in to frequencies beyond our material world, change your brain circuitry and chemistry to access transcendent levels of awareness, and transform your biology to enable profound healing? Dr Joe Dispenza draws on up-to-the-minute research in neuroscience, epigenetics, psychoneuroimmunology, neurocardiology, electromagnetism and quantum physics to show how human transformation and change takes place and what it can mean for our lives. *Becoming Supernatural* explores how to free yourself from the past by reconditioning your body to a new mind and how to shift your awareness into the quantum field of infinite possibilities.

- *Breaking the Habit of Being Yourself: How to Lose Your Mind and Create a New One* by Dr Joe Dispenza. (Hay House Inc. 2013) Available in print and Kindle.

  You are not doomed by your genes and hardwired to be a certain way for the rest of your life. A new science is emerging that empowers all human beings to create the reality they choose. In *Breaking the Habit of Being Yourself* Dr Joe Dispenza combines the fields of quantum physics, neuroscience, brain chemistry, biology and genetics to show you what is truly possible. You will not only be given the necessary knowledge to change any aspect of yourself, but also be taught the step-by-step tools to apply what you learn to make measurable changes in any area of your life.

- *Courageous Dreaming: How Shamans Dream the World into Being* by Alberto Villoldo. (Hay House Inc. 2009) Available in print and Kindle.

  Modern physics tells us that we're dreaming the world into being with every thought. *Courageous Dreaming* tells us how to dream our world with power and grace. The ancient shamans of the Americas understood that we are not only creating our experience of the world but are dreaming up the very nature of reality itself, that is, 'life is but a dream'. When you don't dream your life, you have to settle for the nightmare being dreamed by others. This book shows how to wake up from the collective nightmare and begin to dream a life of courage and grace – a sacred dream that shamans throughout time have known and served. Alberto Villoldo reveals ancient wisdom teachings that explain how to birth reality from the invisible matrix of creation and how we can interact with this matrix to dream a life of peace, health and abundance. He shows us that courage is all that is required to create the joy we desire!

- *Creative Visualization: Use the Power of Your Imagination to Create What You Want in Your Life* by Shakti Gawain. (New World Library 2016) Available in print and Kindle.

This classic guide is filled with meditations, exercises and techniques that can help you to use the power of your imagination to create what you want in your life, change negative habit patterns, improve self-esteem, reach career goals, increase prosperity, develop creativity, increase vitality, improve your health, experience deep relaxation and much more.

- *E-Squared: Nine Do-It-Yourself Energy Experiments That Prove Your Thoughts Create Your Reality* by Pam Grout. (Hay House Inc. 2013) Available in print and Kindle.

E-Squared could best be described as a lab manual with simple experiments that prove reality is malleable, consciousness trumps matter and you shape your life with your mind.

- *Evolve Your Brian: The Science of Changing Your Mind* by Dr Joe Dispenza. (Health Communications Inc. 2008) Available in print and Kindle.

Evolve Your Brain connects the subjects of thought and consciousness with the brain, the mind and the body. Grounded in science, this book explores how the brain works and why it perpetuates the same behaviour patterns over and over. Most importantly, it will help you understand how to use more of your brain to fulfill your potential.

- *Excuse Me, Your Life is Waiting: The Astonishing Power of Feelings* by Lynn Grabhorn. (Hampton Roads Publishing 2009) Available in print and Kindle.

  Feelings, the most unconscious part of us, actually create and mould every moment of every day in our lives. They, not positive thinking, or sweat and strain, or good or bad luck, make our lives what they are. *Excuse Me, Your Life is Waiting* finally clarifies why most of our dreams have never materialised, why we have lived with all-too-empty bank accounts, tough relationships, failing health and spiritually unfulfilling lives. The key to getting back on the right track is simple: focus inward on what it would feel like to have it all go right. And it will.

- *Heal Your Body: The Mental Causes for Physical Illness and the Metaphysical Way to Overcome Them* by Louise L. Hay. (Hay House Inc. 1984) Available in print and Kindle.

  If you suffer from physical ailments, you'll find this 'little blue book' to be a handy affirmation resource when it comes time to making your mind movie. It offers positive new thought patterns to replace negative emotions. It includes an alphabetical chart of physical ailments, the problem causes and healing affirmations to help you eliminate old patterns.

- *Heart Intelligence: Connecting with the Intuitive Guidance of the Heart* by Doc Childre, Howard Martin, Deborah Rozman and Rollin McCraty. (Waterfront Digital Press 2016) Available in print and Kindle.

  Heart Intelligence provides readers with a new, high-definition picture of the energetic heart as a unifying, creative, intuitive intelligence that we can learn to draw on for moment-to-moment guidance. *Heart Intelligence* links the physical heart to the spiritual (energetic) heart. Through its extensive communication with the brain and body, the heart is intimately involved in how we think, feel and respond to the world. This book provides information and simple practices for accessing our heart's intuitive guidance to connect with our highest choices for better outcomes.

- *PSYCH-K®: The Missing Peace in Your Life!* by Robert M Williams. (Myrddin Publications 2004) Available in print and Kindle.

Your reality is created by your beliefs. These beliefs, usually subconscious, are often the result of lifelong programming and represent a powerful influence on human behaviour. It is self-defeating behaviours we wish to change. Often the most effective way to change a behaviour is to change the subconscious belief(s) that support it.

Based on years of split-brain research, also known as Brain Dominance Theory, PSYCH-K® provides a variety of ways to quickly identify and transform beliefs that 'sabotage' you into beliefs that 'support' you, in any area of your life. This book will help the reader discover: why you don't always do the right thing, even when you know the right thing to do; why trying smarter is better than trying harder; and why changing yourself can change the world. The book is a companion to the PSYCH-K® experiential workshops where participants learn specific techniques for changing self-limiting beliefs. The book provides the foundational philosophy and science behind this revolutionary process.

- *Secrets of the Lost Mode of Prayer: The Hidden Power of Beauty, Blessing, Wisdom and Hurt* by Gregg Braden. (Hay House Inc. 2006) Available in print and Kindle.

In this book, Gregg Braden describes what ancient traditions believed to be the most powerful force in the Universe – the power of prayer. However, this ancient form of prayer has no words or outward expressions. Instead, it is based solely on feeling.

- *The Artist's Way: A Spiritual Path to Higher Creativity* by Julia Cameron. (Souvenir Press 2012) Available in print and Kindle.

  The Artist's Way is an international bestseller that will take you on a 12-week journey of self-discovery. It contains hundreds of highly effective exercises, many of which are designed to help you explore who you really are and what inspires you.

- *The Biology of Belief: Unleashing the Power of Consciousness, Matter and Miracles* by Dr Bruce H. Lipton. (Hay House Inc. 2016) Available in print.

  This book will forever change how you think about your own thinking. Stunning new scientific discoveries about the biochemical effects of the brain's functioning show that all the cells in your body are affected by your thoughts. Dr Bruce Lipton, a renowned cell biologist, describes the precise molecular pathways through which this occurs. Using simple language, illustrations, humour and everyday examples, he demonstrates how the new science of Epigenetics is revolutionising our understanding of the link between mind and matter and the profound effects it has on our personal lives and the collective life of our species.

- *The Bond: How to Fix Your Falling-Down World* by Lynne McTaggart. (Pub: Atria Books; Reprint edition; 2012) Available in print and Kindle.

  Building on her bestseller, *The Intention Experiment*, Lynne McTaggart's groundbreaking work, *The Bond*, reveals the latest science to prove that we are all connected, that collaboration trumps competition and that empathy is essential.

- *The Divine Matrix: Bridging Time, Space, Miracles and Beliefs* by Gregg Braden (Hay House Inc. 2008) Available in print and Kindle.

  Between 1993 and 2000, a series of groundbreaking experiments revealed dramatic evidence of a web of energy that connects everything in our lives and our world – *the Divine Matrix*. From the healing of our bodies to the success of our careers, relationships and the peace between nations, this new evidence demonstrates that we each hold the power to speak directly to a force that links all of creation. What would it mean to discover that the power to create joy, to heal suffering and bring peace to nations lives inside you? How differently would you live if you knew how to use this power each day of your life? Join Gregg Braden on this extraordinary journey bridging science, spirituality and miracles through the language of *The Divine Matrix*.

- *The Field: The Quest for the Secret Force of the Universe* by Lynne McTaggart. (Pub: Harper Perennial; Updated ed; 2008) Available in print.

  The Field establishes a new biological paradigm: it proves that our body extends electromagnetically beyond ourselves and our physical body. It is within this field that we can find a remarkable new way of looking at health, sickness, memory, will, creativity, intuition, the soul, consciousness and spirituality. *The Field* helps to bridge the gap that has opened up between mind and matter, between us and the cosmos. Original, well-researched and well-documented by distinguished sources, this is the mind/body book for a new millennium.

- *The Intention Experiment: Use Your Thoughts to Change the World* by Lynne McTaggart. (Pub: Thorsons/Element; 2008) Available in print and Kindle.

  In *The Intention Experiment*, Lynne McTaggart joins forces with a team of international, renowned scientists to test the effects of focused group intention on scientifically quantifiable targets – animal, plant and human.

- *The Isaiah Effect: Decoding the Lost Science of Prayer and Prophecy* by Gregg Braden. (Harmony 2001) Available in print.

  Reading *The Isaiah Effect* helped me understand that 'feeling' is the activating force of a prayer, rather than the words themselves. Using principles recognised only recently in quantum physics, Gregg demonstrates how Isaiah's non-religious, non-denominational form of prayer transcends time and distance to bring healing to our bodies and peace in the nations of our modern world.

- *The Power of Eight: Harnessing the Miraculous Energies of a Small Group to Heal Others, Your Life, and the World* by Lynne McTaggart. (Pub: Atria Books; Reprint edition; 2018) Available in print and Kindle.

  Drawing on hundreds of case studies, the latest brain research and dozens of McTaggart's own university studies, *The Power of Eight* provides solid evidence showing that there is such a thing as a collective consciousness. Now you can learn to use it and unleash the power you hold inside of you to heal your own life, with help from this riveting, highly accessible book.

- *The Power of Intention: Learning to Co-create Your World Your Way* by Dr Wayne W. Dyer. (Hay House Inc. 2005) Available in print and Kindle.

  Dr Wayne W. Dyer has researched intention as a force in the Universe that allows the act of creation to take place. This book explores intention – not as something you do but as an energy that you're a part of. We're all intended here through the invisible power of intention. This is the first book to look at intention as a field of energy you can access to begin co-creating your life.

- *The Power of Your Subconscious Mind* by Dr Joseph Murphy. (Wilder Publications 2008) Available in print and Kindle.

  The Power of Your Subconscious Mind gives you the tools you will need to unlock the awesome powers of your subconscious mind. You can improve your relationships, your finances and your physical well-being. Once you learn how to use this unbelievably powerful force, there is nothing you will not be able to accomplish.

- *The Source: The Secrets of the Universe, the Science of the Brain* by Dr Tara Swart. (Penguin 2020) Available in print and Kindle.

  For the first time, Dr Tara Swart, a neuroscientist and senior lecturer at MIT, reveals the surprising science that supports The Law of Attraction as an effective tool for self-discovery and offers a guide to discovering your authentic self to access your best life now.

  Dr Swart reveals how and why manifestation and visualisation actually work by offering the latest breakthroughs in neuroscience and behavioural psychology, including lessons in neuroplasticity, magnetism, emotional and logical thinking, and even hydration, self-care and relaxation.

- *The Spontaneous Healing of Belief: Shattering the Paradigm of False Limits* by Gregg Braden. (Hay House Inc. 2008) Available in print and Kindle.

  A growing body of scientific evidence suggests that our Universe works like a huge computer based in consciousness. Just as everyday computers use a language to create results, the Universe's consciousness computer code is based in the language of human *emotion* and focused *belief*. Knowing that belief is our reality-maker, the way we think of ourselves and our world is now more important than ever!

- *The Success Principles: How to Get from Where You Are to Where You Want to Be* by Jack Canfield with Janet Switzer. (William Morrow Paperbacks 2015) Available in print and Kindle.

  The Success Principles teaches you how to increase your confidence, tackle daily challenges, live with passion and purpose and realise all your ambitions. Filled with memorable and inspiring stories of CEOs, world-class athletes, celebrities and everyday people, it spells out the 64 timeless principles used by successful men and women throughout history – proven principles and strategies that can be adapted for your own life. Practised every day, these principles will change your life beyond your wildest dreams.

- *You Are the Placebo: Making Your Mind Matter* by Dr Joe Dispenza. (Hay House Inc. 2015) Available in print and Kindle.

  Is it possible to heal by thought alone, without drugs or surgery? The truth is that it happens more often than you might expect. Dr Joe Dispenza shares numerous documented cases of those who reversed cancer, heart disease, depression, crippling arthritis and even the tremors of Parkinson's disease by believing in a placebo. Similarly, Dr Joe tells of how others have gotten sick and even died as the victims of a hex or voodoo curse – or after being misdiagnosed with a fatal illness. Belief can be so strong that pharmaceutical companies use double and triple-blind randomised studied to try to exclude the power of the mind over the body when evaluating new drugs.

  You Are the Placebo combines the latest research in neuroscience, biology, psychology, hypnosis, behavioural conditioning and quantum physics to demystify the workings of the placebo effect and show how the seemingly impossible can become possible.

- *You'll See It When You Believe It: The Way to Your Personal Transformation* by Dr Wayne W. Dyer. (William Morrow & Co 1989) Available in print and Kindle.

  Psychotherapist Dr Wayne Dyer shows how to improve your quality of life by tapping into the power that lies within you and using constructive thinking to direct the course of your own destiny. *You'll See It When You Believe It* demonstrates that through belief you can make your life anything you want it to be.

- *Wishes Fulfilled: Mastering the Art of Manifesting* by Dr Wayne W. Dyer. (Hay House Inc. 2013) Available in print and Kindle.

  This book is dedicated to your mastery of the art of realising all your desires. The greatest gift you have been given is the gift of your imagination. Everything that now exists was once imagined. And everything that will ever exist must first be imagined.

  Wishes Fulfilled is designed to take you on a voyage of discovery, wherein you can begin to tap into the amazing manifesting powers that you possess within you and create a life in which all that you imagine for yourself becomes a present fact.

RECOMMENDED LISTENING

Audible

Audible is a good resource for listening material. Because of the amount of audio material I devour, I find a monthly Audible subscription very cost effective. As a Gold Member, you receive your first audiobook for free and then receive one credit each month to download one audiobook of your choice. This membership also includes discounts on audiobooks, access to member-exclusive sales and Audible's Great Listen Guarantee, which allows you to swap the book you've purchased for another if you don't like it. It's slightly cheaper if you subscribe annually.

Below is a list of audio books to get you started. *Note: The description for each is already provided in the reading list above. Unless indicated, the audio book contains all the original content of the book.*

- *Becoming Supernatural: How Common People Are Doing the Uncommon* by Dr Joe Dispenza, narrated by Adam Boyce. (Author's Republic 2020)

- *Breaking the Habit of Being Yourself: How to Lose Your Mind and Create a New One* by Dr Joe Dispenza, narrated by Adam Boyce. (Author's Republic 2020)

- *Creative Visualization: Use the Power of Your Imagination to Create What You Want in Your Life* by Shakti Gawain, narrated by Shakti Gawain. (New World Library 1999)

- *E-Squared: Nine Do-It-Yourself Energy Experiments That Prove Your Thoughts Create Your Reality* by Pam Grout, narrated by Pam Grout. (Hay House 2014)

- *Evolve Your Brian: The Science of Changing Your Mind* by Dr Joe Dispenza, narrated by Sean Runnette. (Tantor Audio 2017)

- *Excuse Me, Your Life is Waiting: The Astonishing Power of Feelings* by Lynn Grabhorn, narrated by Susan Hanfield. (Dreamscape Media 2021)

- *Heal Your Body: The Mental Causes for Physical Illness and the Metaphysical Way to Over Come Them* by Louise L. Hay, narrated by Stevie Zimmerman. (Louise Hay 2018)

- *Living the Field: Tapping into the Secret Force of the Universe is a speech* by Lynne McTaggart. (Sounds True 2012).

  Living the Field presents a full-length audio workshop about using the scientific discoveries of the quantum age to supercharge your life, health and consciousness.

- *Living with Intention: The Science of Using Thoughts to Change Your Life and the World is a speech* by Lynne McTaggart. (Sounds True 2012)

  Is intention simply wishful thinking or is it a force that can actually change the world around you? Nobody has made a more comprehensive investigation of the power of the mind to influence the Universe than Lynne McTaggart. Her conclusion: Thought does shape reality, but much depends on how skilfully the thinker can use his or her intention. With *Living with Intention*, this groundbreaking author builds upon her findings from *The Field* to explore what makes mind over matter work, what can interfere with its effectiveness, and how you can use focused thought to enhance your life, help those around you and transform your world.

- *The Biology of Belief: Unleashing the Power of Consciousness, Matter and Miracles* by Dr Bruce H. Lipton, narrated by Dr Bruce H. Lipton. (Sounds True 2006) *Note: This audio is a shortened version of the book.*

- *The Divine Matrix: Bridging Time, Space, Miracles and Beliefs* by Gregg Braden, narrated by Gregg Braden. (Hay House Inc. 2008) *Note: This audio is a shortened version of the book.*

- *The Field: The Quest for the Secret Force of the Universe is a speech* by Lynne McTaggart. (Sounds True 2007)

  Lynne McTaggart takes listeners on a journey into an exciting area of science, called the 'Zero-Point Field', that could be the key to understanding 'supernatural' forces, healing energy and the natural state of consciousness.

- *The Isaiah Effect: Decoding the Lost Science of Prayer and Prophecy is a speech* by Gregg Braden. (Sounds True 2001)

  The Great Isaiah Scroll: Does it hold the secrets to changing your life? In Jerusalem, within the Shrine of the Book Museum, resides the Great Isaiah Scroll – the most precious artifact of the Dead Sea Scrolls. So valuable is this scripture that extraordinary measures have been taken to safeguard it against any natural disaster or act of war. Why is this single document, lost to humanity for more than 2000 years, so crucial to modern scholars and mystics? In *The Isaiah Effect*, best-selling author Gregg Braden takes us on an investigation into this ancient Essene scripture, to reveal a set of inner tools capable of altering the destiny of human civilisation.

- *The Power of Eight: Harnessing the Miraculous Energies of a Small Group to Heal Others, Your Life and the World* by Lynne McTaggart, narrated by Gabra Zackmann. (Simon & Schuster Audio 2017)

- *The Power of Intention: Learning to Co-create Your World Your Way* by Dr Wayne W. Dyer, narrated by Dr Wayne W. Dyer. (Hay House Inc. 2004) *Note: This audio is a shortened version of the book.*

- *The Power of Your Subconscious Mind* by Dr Joseph Murphy, narrated by Clay Lomakayu. (Majestic 2015)

- *The Source: The Secrets of the Universe, the Science of the Brain* by Dr Tara Swart, narrated by Dr Tara Swart. (Random House Audiobook 2019)

- *The Spontaneous Healing of Belief: Shattering the Paradigm of False Limits* by Gregg Braden, narrated by Gregg Braden (Random House Audiobook 2014)

- *The Success Principles: How to Get from Where You Are to Where You Want to Be* by Jack Canfield with Janet Switzer, narrated by Jack Canfield. (HarperCollins Publishers Limited 2012) *Note: This audio is a shortened version of the book.*

- *You Are the Placebo: Making Your Mind Matter* by Dr Joe Dispenza, narrated by Adam Boyce. (Encephalon LLC 2020)

- *You'll See It When You Believe It: The Way to Your Personal Transformation* by Dr Wayne W. Dyer, narrated by Dr Wayne W. Dyer. (Hay House 2019)

- *Wishes Fulfilled: Mastering the Art of Manifesting* by Dr Wayne W. Dyer, narrated by Dr Wayne W. Dyer. (Hay House 2012)

Hay House Summits

I recommend attending the summits that Hay House regularly present. These online events are free to join and provide access to intimate conversations with the world's leading personal transformation experts. You can get a taste by listening to the mini weekly lessons offered by the *Hay House World Summit Podcast*. To learn more, visit the Hay House website in your region and subscribe to be notified of their upcoming summits:

- Australia – www.hayhouse.com.au
- India – www.hayhouse.co.in
- UK – www.hayhouse.co.uk
- USA – www.hayhouse.com

Podcasts

A podcast is a method of broadcasting audio (and video) files. You can download and listen to podcasts on any smart device. But first you'll need to download a podcast app such as these:

- Podcasts (free, only available for Apple products)
- Pocket Casts (one-off fee to purchase the app)
- Spotify (monthly subscription fee).

When you find a favourite podcast, you can receive new podcasts automatically by subscribing. In the meantime, here are a few suggestions to get you started:

- *Aubrey Marcus Podcast*

  Founder of Onnit and modern philosopher, Aubrey Marcus, asks the important questions: *How do we find our purpose, wake up to who we truly are, have a few more laughs and human-being a little better?* The Aubrey Marcus Podcasts bring in world-class quests from the fields of athletics, health, business, fitness, science, relationship and spirituality, and asks them to open up to the failures and successes that define their wisdom and character.

- *Cleaning up the Mental Mess*

  Dr Caroline Leaf is a cognitive neuroscientist, author, and mental health and mind expert. Whether you are struggling in your personal life or simply want to understand and use your mind to live your best life, this podcast will provide you with practical and scientific tips and tools to help you take back control over your mental, emotional and physical health.

- *Expanded*

  Hosted by Lacy Phillips and co-host Jessica Jill, *Expanded* is a leading manifestation podcast. Their goal is to normalise the practices of manifestation and empower you to get into the driver's seat of your life in order to manifest the experiences, relationships and things that most align with your authenticity.

- *Good Life Project*

  Inspirational, intimate and disarmingly unfiltered conversations about living a fully engaged, fiercely connected and meaning-drenched life. From iconic world-shakers like Elizabeth Gilbert, Sir Ken Robinson, Seth Godin and Gretchen Rubin to everyday guests, every story matters.

- *Hay House World Summit*

  Offers you weekly mini lessons as a taste of what you can hear during the annual You Can Heal Your Life Summit.

- *Hay House Live!*

  Enjoy insightful and inspiring lectures from *Hay House Live!* events featuring leading experts in the fields of alternative health, nutrition, intuitive medicine, psychology, spirituality, success and personal development. This podcast program will help you get motivated to live your best life possible and open your mind to some new ideas.

- *Living the New Science*

  Join international bestselling author Lynne McTaggart as she shares some of her greatest discoveries and little-known secrets on the New Science and how to 'live' it. You'll learn how to extend your human potential and how to use your thoughts to heal.

- *Mindvalley*

  Mindvalley is the world's leading personal growth education company with a mission to teach wisdom and transformation ideas that our education system ignores. The Mindvalley podcast brings the best minds under one roof to discuss powerful ideas in personal growth for mind, body, spirit and work. Get results that stick.

- *Oprah's Super Soul Conversations*

  Awaken to discover and connect the deeper meaning of the world around you with *Super Soul*. Hear Oprah's personal selection of her interviews with thought leaders, best-selling authors, spiritual luminaries, and health and wellness experts. All designed to light you up, guide you through life's big questions and help bring you closer to your best self.

- *TED Radio Hour*

  The *TED Radio Hour* is a journey through fascinating ideas: astonishing inventions, fresh approaches to old problems, and new ways to think and create. Based on talks given by riveting speakers on the world-renowned TED stage, each show is centred on a common theme such as the source of happiness, crowed-sourcing innovation, power shifts or inexplicable connections. The *TED Radio Hour* is hosted by Guy Raz and is a co-production of NPR and TED.

- *The Tony Robbins Podcast*

  Why live an ordinary life when you can live an extraordinary one? In this podcast, Tony Robbins shares proven strategies and tactics so you can achieve massive results in your business, relationships, health and finances. In addition to excerpts from his signature events and other exclusive, never-before-released audio content, Tony and his team also conduct deeply insightful interviews with the most prominent masterminds and experts on the global stage.

RECOMMENDED VIEWING

YouTube

I search *YouTube* for lectures by my favourite teachers for other sources of a morning and bedtime inspiration. These of course are free.

TED Talks

- *How I Visualised My Dreams into Reality* by Maria Rahajeng (TEDxYouth@SWA)

  www.youtube.com/watch?v=8QTP-QOsC0o

  E! News host and inspirational leader, Maria Rahajeng, shares how she drew a dream board to help her visualise what she wanted to be when she grew up. She explains how all the intentions she sketched out on the vision board she made as a sixteen-year-old had come to fruition by the time she reached her late twenties.

- *If Your Life is Your Biggest Project, Why Not Design It?* by Ayse Birsel (TEDxCannes)

  www.youtube.com/watch?v=-p87nJ4XQHY

  Award-winning industrial designer, Ayse Birsel, believes that if you have the desire to explore your life from a new point of view, think about it proactively and change it creatively, there is a way to design the life you love. In this TEDx talk she outlines her four-step process for designing an original life that reflects your values and looks, feels and even smells like you. Her methodology involves thinking differently, playfully and optimistically about your life. Ayse says that by applying creative processes and design principles, such as sketching, model making and visualisation, you bring your desired reality into form.

- *Imagination Changes Everything* by Patti Dobrowolski (TEDxSacramentoSalon)

  www.youtube.com/watch?v=-wuBFBnCg3c

  Patti Dobrowolski, author of *Drawing Solutions*, explains how visual goal setting will change your life. She believes that when you dream of a desired reality, then draw a picture of it, add all the qualities and characteristics you want to experience, and enter into that world and play there, it will come to be. You don't need to worry about how to get there, she says. Life will fill in the blanks.

- *The Hidden Code for Transforming Dreams Into Reality* by Mary Morrissey (TEDxWilmingtonWomen)

  www.youtube.com/watch?v=UPoTsudFF4Y

  What could your ideal life look like one year from today? Throughout her life, life coach and best-selling author Mary Morrissey was able to improve her results, no matter how difficult the challenge. Through interactions with thousands of leaders including the Dalai Lama, Nelson Mandela and delegates to the United Nations, Mary explains how to advance confidently in the direction of your dreams using the power of imagination.

- *The Power of Visualisation* by Ashanti Johnson (TEDxWillowCreek)

  www.youtube.com/watch?v=S95-9-VuB0U

  Every day for one year, Ashanti Johnson would daydream about her business without doubt, fear or judgement. Little did she know that she was visualising, and the more she allowed the unfolding, it intensified until it became a full-blown reality. Ashanti is now a Fitness Instructor and the Owner of fitness brand 360.Mind.Body.Soul, which combines physical fitness with mental fitness. As a frequent speaker, she loves to share the latest research about the connection and disconnection between mind, body and soul.

- *The Secret Imagination of Elite Performers* by Charlie Unwin (TEDxHolyhead)

  www.youtube.com/watch?v=FK3STeyLUEU

  In a world where success and failure can be measured so publicly, former Army Officer and Olympic Psychologist Charlie Unwin explores in this fascinating talk the intuitive qualities and mental skills that separate high achievers from the rest. In doing so, he draws upon his own experience to expose the paradox of a so-called 'winning mindset' and suggests how we could all be applying the most effective tool in sport psychology to enrich our everyday life.

- *The Secret to Transforming your Dream into Reality* by Dima Ghawi (TEDxSpringHillCollege)

  https://www.youtube.com/watch?v=UPoTsudFF4Y

  In this TEDx talk, motivational speaker and author Dima Ghawi transports the audience decades back to her grandmother's kitchen in the Middle East where she received a gift that fuelled her lifelong determination. Through personal narratives, Dima shares the power of transforming a dream into a belief by first making it tangible, and then harnessing the desire and determination to take action to make it a reality.

Gaia

Gaia is a media network with an online library comprising of more than 8000 ad-free wellness and mind-expanding videos, award-winning documentaries and inspirational films. It is one of my favourite resources for growth and features a number of my teachers. Gaia offers three levels of membership depending on your budget. I find the Gaia Annual Plan to be the most cost effective. Below are a few favourites to get you started:

Interviews

- *64 Powerful Principles of Success* with Jack Canfield (Inspirations with Lisa Garr; March 2015; Season 7, Episode 29)

  'Live big' is Jack Canfield's motto. It's what helped him stay inspired after 144 publishers turned him down for the *Chicken Soup for the Soul Series*. This was the driving force behind creating the franchise that to date has more than 500 million copies in print worldwide. In this inspiring interview, Jack discusses elements of his latest book, *The Success Principles*, which offers readers 64 powerful principles for success.

- *Becoming Supernatural* with Joe Dispenza (Beyond Belief with George Noory; November 2018; Season 10, Episode 8)

  What does it mean to become supernatural? Dr Joe Dispenza has travelled the world to study people who have spontaneously healed from major illnesses in order to find ways that all of us can use to make significant changes in our wellbeing. He has uncovered the connection between body and mind, whereby changes in your personality can create changes in your personal reality. He shares techniques that we can use to change our emotional states and perceptions, which reflect as positive changes in the body and states of wellbeing.

- *Changing Your Reality* with Niurka (Inspirations with Lisa Garr; January 2014; Season 5, Episode 12)

  You are what you think. So says Niurka, a professional speaker and transformational leader. Niurka's teachings are based on the principle that the quality of your life mirrors the quality of the questions you pose. In this motivating interview, she shares how you can change your questions to change your reality.

- *Coherence of HeartMath* (Healing Matrix with Sue Morter; November 2019; Season 3, Episode 13)

  Bridging humanity with science, HeartMath helps us incorporate the heart's intelligence into our day-to-day experiences. Deborah Rozman, founding executive director of HeartMath, offers us a quick introduction to some of the most powerful techniques that can help you to find a nice internal rhythm between heart and mind, and return you to a state of coherence throughout your whole life. What she offers can help us move from personal coherence, within the body, to being energetically interconnected with others by building social coherence.

- *Creating the HeartMath Connection* (Inspirations with Lisa Garr; 2011 Season 1, Episode 1)

  In this episode, originally broadcast live, Howard Martin from HeartMath answers viewer questions on reducing stress and the science of creating a deep connection between the heart and brain. We explore the very fabric of consciousness, how it is changing and the emotional reactions to our perceptions of stress. All of this is reflected in an electromagnetic field that surrounds the body, which can be detected and measured.

- *Five Levels of Manifestation* with Pam Oslie (Inspirations with Lisa Garr; June 2019; Season 10, Episode 15)

  We are far more powerful than we think. Imagine if you could manifest what you desire instantly. Author, consultant and psychic intuitive Pam Oslie not only insists it can be done but also reveals how she's been doing it. She has dramatic stories from experimenting with parallel Universes, creating realities that don't seem possible. She explains the five levels of manifestation and how we can bring the things we desire in life closer to us with a daily practice.

- Howard Martin on the *HeartMath Solution for Stress* (Inspirations with Lisa Garr; 2011 Season 1, Episode 2)

  Howard Martin is Executive Vice President of HeartMath, a program he helped Doc Childre found in 1991. HeartMath is a powerful research-based technique that helps establish heart-based living by inspiring people to connect with the intelligence and guidance of their own hearts. Where stress creates chaos and disharmony in the body, the HeartMath technique is a way to manage stress, leading to a harmonious state called coherence, which, as Howard demonstrates, can be both measured and monitored.

- Jeff Fannin on *You're Not Your Brain* (Healing Matrix with Regina Meredith; January 2013; Season 1, Episode 8)

  Can you learn to manage your mind? Yes, says brain performance expert Dr Jeffrey Fannin of the Centre for Cognitive Enhancement, who discusses the latest in neurofeedback, brain mapping and PSYCH-K®.

- Joe Dispenza on *The Power of Changing Your Thinking* (Inspirations with Lisa Garr; February 2012; Season 1, Episode 11)

  Changing ingrained habits is hard. Or is it? Neuroscientist, chiropractor and author Dr Joe Dispenza empowers people to change from the inside out.

- Joe Dispenza on *Breaking the Habit of Being Yourself* (Inspirations with Lisa Garr; February 2012; Season 1, Episode 12)

  When you try to change an old habit, do you wonder why it's so difficult to change? Do you want to learn how to be more positive or resilient, but don't know how? In this eye-opening and potentially life-changing interview, Dr Joe Dispenza explains how our habits are wired into our brains and what we can do about them.

- Lynn McTaggart on the *Power of Intention* (Inspirations with Regina Meredith; July 2012; Season 2, Episode 4)

  Lynne McTaggart shares her understanding of the connectedness of all things and of the power to harness our thoughts and intentions to change the world.

- *Mystery of the Placebo Effect* with Dr Joe Dispenza (Healing Matrix with Regina Meredith; July 2013; Season 1, Episode 34)

  The placebo has had profound healing effects on many people. But do we really need the pill if the healing power is within us? Dr Joe Dispenza delves into the depths of the mind to reveal the connection between belief, perception, energy fields and the mystery of the placebo, as he explains in this stimulating interview with Regina Meredith.

- Rob Williams on *Rebooting Your Brain* (Healing Matrix with Regina Meredith; December 2012; Season 1, Episode 5)

  The key to changing behaviour isn't trying harder; it's trying smarter. Rob Williams, originator of *PSYCH-K®*, shares how to free your mind from self-defeating habits.

- *Stay Inspired: Harmonising Your Heart and Brain* with Gregg Braden (Inspirations with Lisa Garr; May 2016; Season 8, Episode 12)

  When scientific investigation revealed sensory neurites (brain-like cells) in the heart, it confirmed an expanded understanding of the heart's role beyond pumping blood, aligning with what ancient spiritual traditions have maintained all along. In this revealing interview, Gregg Braden explains that you can tune your heart to work together in harmony with your brain. When you do, he adds, some 1400 biochemical reactions occur with, for example, powerful effects on your immune response, along with a great many other benefits.

- *The Art of Living in Your Dreams* with Mike Dooley (Inspirations with Lisa Garr; November 2019; Season 11, Episode 15)

  Do you want to know how to be at the right place at the right time? We can actually control that with our thoughts. Most of us don't get the degree to which this is true, according to best-selling author Mike Dooley. But we choose, in the moment, what to focus on, and it's those thoughts alone that will become the things and events of our life. Now, it doesn't happen overnight. You have to show up every day; you have to deliberately focus on your dreams; you have to turn your thoughts into things with your daily practice. This is how you can fine tune the art of living your dreams.

- *The Field of Infinite Potentiality* with Pam Grout (Inspirations with Lisa Garr; July 2015; Season 7, Episode 34)

  There are many rules we go by in life, but where do they come from? In two of her recent books, best-selling author Pam Grout has codified some of those rules. Each book contains nine do-it-yourself energy experiments that prove your thoughts create your own reality and that manifesting magic and miracles is your full-time gig. Join Pam for this entertaining interview as she explains her belief that the world is abundant and unlimited.

- *The Science of Heart Intelligence* with Howard Martin (Inspirations with Lisa Garr; December 2018; Season 9, Episode 10)

  The heart is doing more than pumping blood, says Howard Martin of HeartMath. The physical heart is an information processing centre in our bodies. There exists a complex nerve system in the heart, which communicates directly to the brain. Research shows that brain function is critically dependent on the information from the heart, and their alignment leads to states of personal, interpersonal and global coherence. Martin brings us up to date on the remarkable research HeartMath is doing in this arena. The spirit of humanity is rising to the occasion, he says, and we are ushering in a new and very different world right in the midst of the old one.

- *Transform Your Personality, Transform Your Life* with Joe Dispenza (Inspirations with Lisa Garr; January 2019; Season 9, Episode 18)

  How can you learn to break your addiction to a life you don't even like? If you transform your personality, you can transform your life, and that transformation can lead to a life that is nothing short of miraculous. Dr Joe Dispenza reveals how we get trapped in our habitual emotional responses, so much so that by the time we're 35 years old we're a set of memorised programs. In clear language, based on his years of scientific research, he explains that your personality is made up of how you think, how you act and how you feel. If you change those elements you can change your personality. Wouldn't you rather fall in love with your future?

- *You Are the Placebo* with Joe Dispenza (Inspirations with Lisa Garr; June 2014; Season 6, Episode 16)

  Can people overcome habits, illness and disease through the power of thought? Maybe so, says Dr Joe Dispenza, D.C. In his most recent independent research, Dispenza observed that subjects were able to change their state of being through thought alone. Believe it or not, you are the placebo. In this interview taped live at the I Can Do It event in Denver, Colorado, Dispenza shares some of his eye-opening findings with host Lisa Garr.

Series

- *Inner Evolution*

  Dr Bruce Lipton, Ph.D., a pioneer in the field of epigenetics, takes us deep within the structures of cells and into the energy of the quantum realms, to reveal the secret mechanisms connecting consciousness with well-being. In this groundbreaking series, you will come to understand that you are not your genes. Your genetic expression is directly determined by your environment and, more importantly, your perception of that environment.

What you will discover is a scientific approach to understanding the spiritual connection that affects every part of the body. This will empower you to take back control over your genetic blueprint, the way your body responds to the environment and achieve an inner evolution through biological change.

- *Missing Links*

Explore the deep truths of our origin, history, destiny and fate with celebrated author and luminary Gregg Braden.

Season One: Connect science and spirituality to reveal a new understanding of humanity's history, the origins of civilization and the power of our heart's intelligence.

Season Two: Are we living in a virtual reality? Discover the societal and spiritual implications that arise when we recognise our world as an artificially constructed computer simulation.

Season Three: Discover the Divine Matrix, how it influences you and how you can influence it. This could dramatically improve your life, your wellbeing and the lives of all those around you. *Season Three* ends with three inspirational conversations between Gregg Braden and Bruce Lipton.

- *Rewired*

Dr Joe Dispenza brings together his many years of research into the brain and human biology to present the latest findings on what is humanly possible for creating massive transformation in our lives. In fact, you have a supernatural ability to create a new future in your own image. We are not hardwired to be a certain way for the rest of our lives, nor are we doomed by our genes.

Tune in to this epic series as Dr Dispenza reveals the secret formulas for rewiring your brain and building coherence with your being, so that you can move from thinking to doing to being, as a new person in a new future that you have intentionally created.

- *The HeartMath Experience*

  Connect with the heart of who you truly are. Learn from an inspiring experiential program that offers new insights and practical techniques to help you respond to day-to-day challenges with more ease and composure.

  Unlock your heart's natural intuitive guidance. Better manage stressful emotions. Increase resilience. Hear from experts and master trainers. Experience five scientifically validated HeartMath techniques for activating your heart power and intelligence. Learn to move from depletion to renewal – from stress to ease – to become who you truly are.

  'Much like electricity changed the outer world, learning to harness the power and intelligence of the heart will change our inner world.' ~ Howard Martin

- *Transcendence*

  What if you could have everything you ever imagined? What if the life of your dreams was already available? Come on a journey to discover the secrets to living a happy and purposeful life. Learn from the world's best on how you can achieve everything you've ever wanted, using what you already have. Get the tools to transcend your limitations, unlock your personal power and achieve elevated states of consciousness to manifest the life you truly desire.

  Season One: Practical and approachable tools to be able to shine light on your life to help you step into your calling, follow your passions and live the life of your dreams.

Season Two: Understand how powerful your thoughts are and how they can shape your life, your relationships and the world around you.

Movies

It's difficult to find movies that focus on the principles presented in this workbook. Below are those I could source. They are not all of the highest quality, but for those who are new to these concepts and prefer to absorb content visually, they cover the fundamentals.

Documentaries

- *Awake in the Dream* (2013)

  Awake in the Dream gently takes its viewers 'by the hand and heart' and guides them into the recognition of their inherent divine creative power. *Awake* transports its message through internationally well-known spiritual leaders, visionaries and scientists, and the radically honest and touching story of the filmmaker herself.

  The film offers astonishing and easy-to-follow answers to the most crucial questions of humanity: *Who are we really?*, *What is the sense of life?*, *How can I find happiness?* Many simple and easy-to-apply tools within the movie allow the audience to find their old sabotaging mechanisms and to transform them.

  Featuring: Arjuna Ardagh, Rudiger Dahlke, Barbara Marx Hubbard, Tom Kenyon, Bruce Lipton, Mooji, Eric Pearl, Catharina Roland, Neale Donald Walsch and Nassim Haramein.

- *Emotion 2.0* (2014)

  Scientists show how emotions affect the physiology of the human body and how replacing negative emotions can improve our health and create abundance, inner peace and loving relationships.

Featuring: Dr Joe Dispenza, Dr Bradley Nelson, Nassim Haramein, Neale Donald Walsh, Sonia Choquette and Don Tolman.

- *Free Solo* (2018)

  Immerse yourself in the experience of Alex Honnold's phenomenal free solo climb up the sheer, 884-metre vertical cliff face of El Capitan in Yosemite National Park. To achieve this incredible feat, without safety ropes, Alex needed to overcome his doubts, fears and negative self-talk by physically and mentally rehearsing the entire climb in his mind, move by move, until his body remembered every crevice.

- Heal (2017)

  Take a scientific and spiritual journey to discover that our thoughts, beliefs and emotions have a huge impact on our health and ability to heal. The latest science reveals that we are not victims of unchangeable genes, nor should we buy into a scary prognosis. The fact is we have more control over our health and life than we have been taught to believe. This film will empower you with a new understanding of the miraculous nature of the human body and the extraordinary healer within us all.

  Heal not only taps into the brilliant minds of leading scientists and spiritual teachers but follows three people on their high-stakes healing journeys. Healing can be extremely complex and deeply personal, but it can also happen spontaneously in a moment. Through these inspiring and emotional stories, we find out what works, what doesn't and why.

  Featuring: Dr Deepak Chopra, Anita Moorjani, Marianne Williamson, Dr Michael Beckwith, Dr Bruce Lipton, Dr Joe Dispenza, Anthony William 'Medical Medium', Dr Bernie Siegel, Gregg Braden, Dr Joan Borysenko, Dr David Hamilton, Dr Kelly

Brogan, Rob Wergin, Dr Kelly Turner, Peter Chrone, Dr Darren Weissman and Dr Jeffrey Thompson.

- *House of Cardin* (2019)

  House of Cardin is an in-depth look at visionary fashion and design icon Pierre Cardin's work and personal life. Combining acute business acumen with an almost unrivalled creation vision, Cardin was a fashion revolutionary whose designs from the 1960s and 1970s still appear modern decades later. In what was perceived as a shocking move at the time, he was the very first designer to branch out from haute couture into ready-to-wear and expand his range to incorporate fashion accessories – all accepted as standard practice today.

- *Manifest: Power of Thought* (2016)

  This movie speaks to the heart of this workbook series and is well worth watching, even purchasing. *Manifest: Power of Thought* is the multi-award-winning documentary that explores how our thoughts impact our lives via four dramatic real-life case studies and insightful commentary by world-leading personal transformation experts.

- *Muhammad Ali: The Greatest* (2016)

  Muhammad Ali always saw himself as the greatest – a gold medal winner and the world champion. His method of trash talking opponents in rhyme affirmed his intentions and sent a very clear message to the Universe. This retrospective documentary charts the rise and fall of Muhammad Ali, considered to be one of the greatest sporting figures of the 20th century.

- *The I Field 2.0* (2019)

  The I Field, directed by Tsipi Raz, brings to the screen 12 experiments in real time to examine the ancient wisdom saying: We are far beyond matter, connected to one another and to the Universe.

Featuring: Gregg Braden, Dr Bruce Lipton, Lynne McTaggart, Dr Todd Ovokaitys, Lee Caroll, Dr Rollin McCraty, Dr Roger Nelson, Professor Carlo Ventura, Professor Konstantin Korotkov and many more.

- *The Power of the Heart* (2014)

  From the director of *The Secret* comes this unparalleled and life-changing film about the astonishing power and intelligence of your heart. Featuring some of the most inspiring and influential icons of our age including Paulo Coelho, Maya Angelou, Deepak Chopra, Isabel Allende and Eckhart Tolle, this film presents fascinating evidence that your heart is much more than a physical organ, and that it can transform your views of money, health, relationships and success.

  The Power of the Heart is an experience that will lead you to uncover – and rediscover – the treasure in your chest.

  Featuring: Maya Angelou, Deepak Chopra, Eckhart Tolle, Paulo Coelho, Mark Nepo, Michael Beckwith, Eckhart Tolle and Jane Goodall.

- *The Secret* (2006)

  While rudimentary in nature, *The Secret* discusses the Law of Attraction and how to use it in your life. It introduces people to the concept that their thoughts may influence not only their actions, but also the experiences that they bring into their lives.

  Featuring: Dr John Demartini, Bob Proctor, Joe Vitale, John Assaraf, Michael Beckwith, Jack Canfield and others.

- *What If? The Movie* (2009)

  Within you sits the power to move mountains, manifest instantly, live in the Divine Reality of unconditional love, and be, do and have everything you could ever want. Why? It's already who you are; you've just learned to limit it.

What If? is an award-winning feature-length documentary film known as the ultimate human potential movie. It speaks on many of the principles discussed in this workbook and is worth watching, even purchasing.

Featuring: Dr Joe Dispenza, Dr Bruce Lipton, Dr Masaru Emoto, Bernie Siegel and Brandon Bays.

Biographies

- *Eddie the Eagle* (2015)

  Inspired by true events, *Eddie the Eagle* is a feel-good story about Michael 'Eddie' Edwards (Taron Egerton), an unlikely but courageous British ski-jumper who never stopped believing in himself, even as an entire nation was counting him out. With the help of a rebellious and charismatic coach (played by Hugh Jackman), Eddie takes on the establishment and wins the hearts of sports fans around the world by making an improbable and historic showing at the 1988 Calgary Winter Olympics. From producers of *Kingsman: The Secret Service*, *Eddie the Eagle* stars Taron Egerton as Eddie, the loveable underdog with a never-say-die attitude.

- *Ride Like a Girl* (2019)

  Michelle Payne is the youngest of ten children of racehorse trainer Paddy Payne. From the time Michelle was a little girl she dreamed of being a jockey and winning the Melbourne Cup, Australia's most prestigious annual Thoroughbred horse race. In 2015, she became the first woman to ride the winner, despite the personal and professional odds stacked against her.

- *You Can Heal Your Life* (2007)

  This entertaining and inspirational movie based on the best-selling book of the same name is hosted by author and teacher Louise L. Hay. This film gives penetrating insights into

Louise's personal story and shows her profound views on the relationship between the mind and the body. Exploring the way that limiting thoughts and ideas control and constrict us, Louise offers us a powerful key to understanding the roots of our physical diseases and discomforts. It also reveals how she applied these concepts to her own emotional, spiritual and professional life.

Drama

- *Chariots of Fire* (2014)

  This movie is based on the true story of two British athletes competing in the 1924 Summer Olympics in Paris. Englishman Harold Abrahams (Ben Cross), who is Jewish, overcomes anti-Semitism and class prejudice in order to compete against the 'Flying Scotsman', Eric Liddell (Ian Charleson), in the 100-metre race.

- *Field of Dreams* (1989)

  An Iowa corn farmer (Kevin Costner), hearing voices, interprets them as a command to build a baseball diamond in his fields. He does, and the 1919 Chicago White Sox come.

- *Stranger than Fiction* (2006)

  Everybody knows that your life is a story. But what if a story was your life? Harold Crick (Will Ferrell) is your average IRS Agent: monotonous, boring and repetitive. But one day this all changes when Harold begins to hear an author inside of his head narrating his life. The narrator is extraordinarily accurate, and Harold recognises the voice as an esteemed author he saw on television. But when the narration reveals that he is going to die, Harold must find the author of the story, and ultimately his life, to convince her to change the ending of the story before it is too late.

- *The Secret: Dare to Dream* (2020)

  A widow (Katie Holmes) struggling to get by meets a stranger (Josh Lucas) who subscribes to a philosophy of positive thinking.

- *What the Bleep Do We (K)now!?* (2004)

  A fictional photographer's quest to spiritually rediscover herself is interspersed with documentary footage of scientists and theologians discussing the philosophical aspects of quantum physics.

  Featuring: Actors: Marlee Matlin and Elaine Hendrix. Interviews: Fred Alan Wolf, Dean Radin, John Hagelin, Candace Pert, Joe Dispenza, Amit Goswami, Jeffrey Satinover, Daniel Monti, David Albert, William Tiller, Miceal Ledwith, Masaru Emoto and Ramtha.

- *What the Bleep!? Down the Rabbit Hole* (2006)

  The concepts of quantum theory and spiritual well-being originally put forth in the 2004 feature *What the Bleep Do We Know?!* are expanded upon in this extended version of the same film, featuring a new opening, a variety of new interviews and three new computer-animation segments.

  If anyone found themselves questioning anything and everything about the reality that surrounds them after viewing the original film, newly shot interviews with scientists Dean Radin and Dr Masaru Emoto, as well as author Lynne McTaggart, help to put the previously presented information into a new context while offering a revealing look at the world we only thought we knew.

  Featuring: Actors: Marlee Matlin and Elaine Hendrix. Interviews: Joe Dispenza, Dean Radin, William Tiller, Fred Alan Wolf, Amit Goswami, J. Z. Knight and Lynne McTaggart.

Family

- *Cool Runnings* (1993)

  Four Jamaicans form their country's first ever bobsled team to compete in the upcoming 1988 Winter Olympics. They enlist the help of a disgraced former Olympic gold winner to reluctantly coach them. However, when they reach Canada, they're treated as outsiders by the other teams, who fear they'll only succeed in embarrassing the sport.

  Cool Runnings is not the true story of the Jamaican Bobsled team; it is inspired by it. Despite that, it does capture the spirit of the team and the derision they faced. In a fun and entertaining way, the filmmakers display the true lesson of the team: if you have a dream, go after it, no matter what anyone else says.

- *Unlocking the Secret* (2008)

  While a little dated, this film investigates and presents insights into how our thoughts and emotions create our reality.

  Featuring: Eme Ikwuakor, Drew Repp, Summer Snover and Elisa Vasquez.

RECOMMENDED EVENTS

If you enjoyed or were at least drawn to *Activity 5*, you might enjoy one of Dr Joe Dispenza's retreats. The format of these events allows participants to retreat from the constant stimulation of their external environment – such as people they know, things they own and their daily routine – and immerse themselves in powerful meditation practices with like-minded people in a supportive environment.

The change in environment and the group energy gained through Dr Joe's retreats help facilitate an even deeper experience when doing the mental rehearsal prescribed in this workbook. Participating in such an event can also stimulate positive memories and associations, which can in turn be helpful for continuing the work.

NOTE FROM THE AUTHOR

I trust you enjoyed the process of imagineering your ultimate future. I'm looking forward to you sharing your vision and hearing about your aha moments!

Feel free to email me or post your thoughts on Facebook, so the *A Guide for Life* community can be inspired and benefit from your insights.

Email: kylie@aguideforlife.com
Facebook: www.facebook.com/aguideforlife